THE CIVIL RIGHTS ERA THROUGH THE EYES OF A CHILD:
THE ROAD TO FREEDOM

I LIVED ON THE OTHER SIDE OF THE LINE

CARLOTTA MARIA SHINN-RUSSELL

SHINN
RUSSELL
BOOKS & PUBLICATIONS

THE CIVIL RIGHTS ERA THROUGH THE EYES OF A CHILD:
THE ROAD TO FREEDOM

I LIVED
ON THE
OTHER SIDE
OF THE
LINE

CARLOTTA MARIA SHINN-RUSSELL

DEDICATION
VI

This book is dedicated to all the unsung heroes that stood with Martin Luther King, Jr., in fear and yet, not fearing, what would happen tomorrow. Those unsung heroes who faced a monster and stood firm in their resolve to enjoy the rights given them by the Constitution of the United States of America, for all people regardless of race, creed, color, or natural origin. Freedom was not free when Abraham Lincoln pinned the Emancipation Proclamation and freed the black race from the cruelest conditions of life "slavery." Those unsung heroes did not just exist in this country, but in other countries as well. There were always helpers that were willing to take up the fight no matter which continent.

The Emancipation Proclamation was one of the greatest speeches ever penned by man. The words set down on paper were the most exhilarating and hope-giving words ever uttered by man. It gave a race of people their first glimpse of freedom, their first breath of fresh air, their first hope to be proud to say they were Americans that could hold their heads high and go anywhere they wanted to, as well as have equal rights to partake in the riches of freedom in the richest country in this world.

Consequently, all too soon the hope of this freedom was being dashed by a single act, of human intolerance. Life in this so-called free society became a mental, emotional and social prison just another form of slavery. Undeservingly, the Negro, was once again being held in slavery of another type namely hatred and intolerance because, of one group of insensitive people with a like ideology, they had just been freed from. No equal rights, no rights at all, citizens still had to run for their lives to stay free or accept sub-human conditions in silence. The taunting words, innuendoes, racial slurs all of this is a form of slavery whether the chains and boundaries are mental or physical, they have the same results, a suppression of a race of people actually who were the backbone of the south. The slaves made the plantation owners wealthy because, they carried the burden in the heat of the day. They did the work.

Shane said, "Her parents spoke with them on many occasions on this topic and discussed in details with their children the "question" of the Negro race being free and having equal rights."

1

V I I

There can never be enough said about Abraham Lincoln, President of the United State. Even adjectives like impressive, brilliant, persistent, caring, imaginative, faithful, loyal, and patriotic cannot begin to describe a man of "such" statue; penning the Emancipation Proclamation was just the beginning of the flood- gates, he opened in 1863. Whether he freed the slaves to help save the union or just freed them because of the humanistic access. He knew without the single act of signing the Emancipation Proclamation that, the black race would never have a chance to live free.

This was just a small part of what he accomplished with his 1542 (4 years and 22) days in office. He was heroic in his efforts to bring the nation together as one "United" States. He was the facilitator of one of the first great movements to unify this country. However, as always, change is hard for man to accept, so there were still those that tried to roundup former slaves and make their slavery continue through the continued use of the lash.

There are always heroes out there, notable or not. One of those notable heroes, Dr. Martin Luther King, Jr. took up the torch for freedom. When he penned the "I Have A Dream" speech his vision was just as apparent and just as vivid, for this country, as Abraham Lincoln's was when he penned the Emancipation Proclamation.

There is always a loss of life in the fight for freedom. The War Between the States was a bloody battle for freedom to change a way of life or way of thinking. Martin Luther King, Jr., fought for freedom to give a "Right of Passage" to a people denied that right for more than four hundred plus years.

The Negro citizens were not allowed the simplest of rights; rights as smile as making free choices for themselves. In this quest for freedom, they sought to be free of chains, both physical and mental, free of lines, whether that choice of lines was mental or physical.

Echoes of slavery ran in the ears of the Negro race. Freedom, for the Negro, was like a handkerchief that is kept in the pockets of the slave owners to be pulled out only for use on a now-and-then basis; it was not a privilege that could be enjoyed daily by the black race.

There were echoes that rang in the 1960's and the years before of a time gone by for more than four hundred years of the stories told of slavery, which never found a home of rest and will never find that place of rest in bondage of any kind. There is a spirit in man that desires to be free and have freedom for all. Bitter pills are hard to swallow no matter the kind, whether it medically or politically. Slavery was a bitter pill that the Negro had to swallow for many centuries.

V I I I

There was an ugly truth hid behind the trees in Georgetown. A secret kept to protect the monster that wreaked havoc on the citizens in this community. Even though danger was there, day and night, the citizens of the black community stood firm and refused to allow fear to reign and rule their lives. After a while, people fear no more instead, morals, the love for life, the love of freedom, and their delineating principles will take over.

As the Emancipation Proclamation was written to break the chains of slavery, so is the will of man to have freedom from the mental chains of slavery is also an unwritten law, this mental law is the unwritten need to be free from all chains of any kind. Freedom is supposed to be free, and not meted out in small amounts.

My husband, Timothy B. Russell, Sr. did not live to see this book come to fruition, but he envisioned it with the conversations we had about the Civil Rights Era. He was supportive of the events being described in this book because it is a very important part of history that sometimes are so vague that some of the events that took place are not spoken of or talked about enough. He believed that only would wounds and scars heal when they are treated. Equality and Justice for all would be the healing factor for this era. Furthermore, this book is also, dedicated, to my husband. His support, love and insight will always be a part of me as a writer.

The 1960's Civil Rights Era was arguably the most difficult and one of the most important events in the growth and history of this country. The 1960's and its events provided a backdrop for a turn of events that would open America's eyes, so we as a country could look at the problems that this country faced with its own citizens and the issues of race.

An era that demanded that, the necessary steps be taken to eliminate the issues of line and race, thereby adopting a different ideology in reference to the issues of lines and races. Adhering and holding to the past for some issues are good, but not for "all". As a rule, when holding to or adhering to those basic laws that gives all men freedom as referred to in The Constitution, when it makes reference to equality for all citizens of this great country, are good principles and ideologies to hold or adhere to.

Chunchula, Alabama was no different from any other small rural community in the 1960's. There was the division of white's and black's naturally that line was there.

The difference that will stand out is the caliber of the people that lived in the black community or at least two that, Shane described so vividly to me. The picture that she painted for me of her father and mother was awe-inspiring.

Not that they were college educated or different from their neighbors in respect to worldly possessions, but they were different in the way they thought. They had different mentalities of how life and the privilege to enjoy freedom from fear and intimidation that this country and its laws provided was to be.

William Washington, Jr. was a six feet four inches tall, one hundred and seventy pounds man who was a mixture of Creek/Cherokee/Irish – who would stand his ground. Elizabeth Washington was a five-feet eleven inches tall woman, also with a mixture of Creek and French who had the same mentality that as her husband William, did. She would stand her ground as well.

Subsequently, both parents saw a line and did not cross it. It was not a race line, but a line of respect for the next man, his right as a citizen and the right to live in peace without fear, intimidation and assault upon his person. William and Elizabeth presented a unified front as far as their feelings about rights, freedoms and people crossing lines.

What Shane said she never understood was, "If there was a line why did the Ku Klux Klan or any other racist or bias person or group of people cross it? This was not a game of hopscotch, where you draw lines and then cross them. This was an operation of a single-edged sword. You make the rules and then break them yourself." This was an okay mentality that, the Ku Klux Klan and other bias individuals operated on. I made the rules and I can break them whenever and however I like. However, the black man, nor any other minority race could neither of the cross lines nor break the rules. Especially, not without some ramification; however, there were no penalties for the rule maker; because, they took a position of ownership of the making and breaking of the rules.

Shane said, "She thought the ideology of making and breaking the rules for one race and not for the other, as an adult. She told me that she thought that everyone should be held to the same standards not just specific groups and not using that time worn attitude that it is "all for some and none for others." There is suffering in this type of thinking and it is usually the underdog, at that point in time, in the sixties, it was the Blackman/Negro race or anyone in the Negro race."

Shane said, "She saw her mother and father stand against almost impossible as well as, dangerous odds, but it bought fruition – their children learned to stand and be counted as well."

Childhood can teach you many things, including fear of people. The point was, Shane parents taught their children to wage a war as they grew, not to fear or live in fear----it is like not eating properly, which can stunt a child's physical growth, fear can stunt mental and emotional growth. Therefore, it was a war of opposing sides. In fact, there were two wars going on in this small quiet community in Chunchula, Alabama. One was the war the Ku Klux Klan was waging with the black community and the other was the war the Washington parents were waging to raise their children and teach them to fight against oppression and fight back to prevent themselves from being the oppressed.

The example that the Washington parents set for their children had a domino effect–it extended to other families in the neighborhood and they too joined the fight. The more warriors you have on the battle field the better the odds. The Washington parent's bravery helped to level the playing field in the Georgetown Community, in Chunchula, anyway.

V I I I I

When I met Shane, she was not very willing to talk about her experiences in the 1960's when she was growing-up. She said, "It is painful still to speak about. There is always that deep-seated apprehension that ties knots in your stomach at the prospect of what could have happened. The situation surrounding the Civil Rights Movement was hard enough without being tense and nerve-racking also. Always, always, you would have to be on your guard and aware of people around you." The early 1960's, according to Shane's account from her mother Elizabeth, "Life in Chunchula was fairly quiet."

The days went by in a lazy way as it would in any rural area in the South. Life was unassuming and quiet for families. Everyone stayed on their own turf and worked their own farms or gardens, or whatever they did for a living." The Civil Rights Movement and the awaking of evil changed the entire dynamics of the community.

There were many actors and players casted on stage in the Civil Rights Movement. There were many actualities and situations presented at those lines drawn between the races. The right to vote, according to the 15th Amendment of the Constitution was granted the Negro. The United States Constitution Amendment XV states in:

Section 1.

The right of citizens of the United States to vote shall not be denied or abridged by the United States or by any state on account of race, color, or previous condition of servitude.

Section 2.

The Congress shall have power to enforce this article by appropriate legislation.

In addition, the peace and safety without fear of assault, according to the 13th Amendment of the Constitution.

13th Amendment to the U.S. Constitution to the Constitution declared that:

"Neither slavery nor involuntary servitude, except as a punishment for crime whereof the party shall have been duly convicted, shall exist within the United States, or any place subject to their jurisdiction."

Formally abolishing slavery in the United States, the 13th Amendment was passed by the Congress on January 31, 1865, and ratified by the states on December 6, 1865.

http://www.loc.gov/rr/program/bib/ourdocs/13thamendment.html, August 24, 2013.

These were simple rights like drinking water out of a fountain, sitting to eat lunch at a lunch counter in downtown Mobile, riding in the front seat of a car or bus. That riding in a car in the back seat drew a color line. Why was it always the back of everything pertaining to the Negro race? As a result, of this, the Negro did not have rights or freedoms of speech, if you did speak out, which some did, there was a huge price to pay. It was okay to say yah sa, or yes'm – but no further. Those lines were always there.

For example, children watching their parents having to hold any comments or actions in response to the insults they suffered at the will of people of another race left a scar of silence. On the other hand, the Ku Klux Klan were loose cannons in the mist of all the movement, words that insulted, showed racial biases, and statements of hate poured from their mouths unchecked.

In short, the Ku Klux Klan seized the opportunity to rage a personal supremacy war on the Southern Blacks populous in Alabama and Mississippi; these two states seemed to catch a heavy brunt of all of the hate lashed at the black race. Learning to hate that much takes a long time and a man or woman would have to had to been indoctrinated with racial and hate biases like a skin is stretched over one's body. Like your skin, you wear it everywhere you go, hate is a mental and emotional thing you wear everywhere you go.

The 1960s Civil Rights Era was alike no other era recorded in the history of America. The nation was involved in finding itself and coming into its own after a daunting twenty-year-stretch between 1940-1960 with the ending of both World War II that had taken place, and the invasive recession that touched everyone's life at the same level. In this wise, there was a war was going on below the surface that would change everybody's world forever.

For the most part, there is nothing wonderful about the years of the Civil Rights Movement, of which, anyone can boast. This movement should have never had to be part of the history of the United States. The Civil Rights Movement left America with a big black eye that came from the refusal of the powers to be to ensure that everyone that crossed the lines and walked upon this free soil called America, have the same rights, equality and justice. As well, these rights, justice and equality should be, assured to all American who lived upon this soil at the same level at the same time.

In particular, the people that suffered through this movement went through some years in their life that left memories engrained in the minds of their adherents, as well as, their ancestors. There are always lines somewhere that people of color cannot cross, even now.

Shane said, "She believes even now that, these lines cover from the Boardroom to the basement a glass ceiling that is being suffered through by the male and female races as they try to pull it down and have the opportunity to work at jobs that once were not accessible and are still not accessible, because of their race."

There was a rumble growing nationwide, but also there was one growing in the rural areas of Mobile County in two small towns called Chunchula and Georgetown. The Chunchula community was predominately black and the Georgetown community was predominately white. Both little towns had sprinkles of black and white around them. Shane said, "I guess you could describe Georgetown as an Oreo Cookie Ice Cream Sundae with hints of Oreo Cookie (the chocolate ones) sprinkle into it and then Chunchula was just the Oreo Cookie with just white cream middle. Either way there was mixture of both races."

In brief, looking at the purpose of the book will give the reader an insight into the reason the author thought it was necessary to document this part of the unrecorded Civil Rights Era.

PURPOSE
V I I I I I

The purpose of this book is to describe in a picture-graphic manner the events as told to her by citizens that lived during that time, who experienced these events personally. This book attempt is to establish a descriptive and effective atmosphere within the time-frame leading up to during and after the Civil Rights Movement. Even though, the Ku Klux Klan operated long before the 1950's and 1960's, the intervening chapters describes the pain, hurt and total disregard for a race of people.

The theme here is freedom, discrimination and segregation of a race of people including looking at facts and events through the periscope of a child's eyes.

For example, this book gives a two-fold look at this era: (1) direct contact with the Ku Klux Klan; and other youth that the era effected; and (2) How the ideology of the Ku Klux Klan had an overflowing effect on how people thought and acted at this period- of- time.

As such, these times in history are, ingrained in the minds of children. It could not be more vivid than if someone took a branding iron and branded it there, not that it is a memory of hate of dislike, but as a vanguard of what was and should not be ever again. Days and events fixed to a child memory, like a brand, puts a permanency there; there is no way of changing it. There is a prescription for change. The only way to change a brand is to put another brand over it that can change the identity. The brand prescription is knowledge and education, desire for change was the only way; you never forget, but with those prescriptions for change; this change will come-to-pass.

The atmosphere, which allowed the growth of the mentality of the Ku Klux Klan was fertilized by the Civil Rights Movement and the lack of lawful constraints. Like the sands of the dry desert, the winds gather the grains and blow them together to make a haunting sound that gives off a chanting sound of uncertainty, so did the sound of the Ku Klux Klan chanting together it also gave a sound of ambiguity. The gathering always meant despair of some kind for someone.

These patterns of cruelty of one race of people over another is history repeating itself, humans do not advance in their treatment of other races, but follow patters like lines drawn in the sands of time. What is it with man and his quest for one race to exert power over another?

For the most part, these types of actions and mentalities were a burden and could became weariness to man. Even nature itself tells us that beast of burdens wears out with being continually overloaded, poked and prodded. Man, only see man in a horizontal, unrealistic manner and through their eyes only; which is not a feasible way to see other people or races. How they feel and what their perceptions are; are the only way man look at each other. If man on a whole saw each other through the eyes of the Maker of Mankind, each of us would be better off.

In particular, Slaves were wealth during the South's hey-day, during the years that the black man worked on the plantation, the slave master managed their property by keeping them in ignorance, which kept them from progressing. Wherefore, so it was with the Ku Klux Klan, not wanting voting rights for the Negro using the same kind of methods of slavery. As a result, this type of fear was passed-down and became a Spiral of Silence. History is a great teacher; whether it is in a positive or negative manner, it is a teacher. With the Ku Klux Klan wanting to deny the Negro the right to vote they added another condition to the already difficulty issues, extinction. The concept of a race becoming extinct is irrational; it became a self-consuming idea for the Ku Klux Klan.

There is an immutable fact; it is that, man or humans are kindred's of each other or they we tied to each other by blood. Man had its beginning together and will have its ending together; from the books of Genesis to Revelations; these facts is written and well documents. In this case, actions followed the apparent thoughts of the Ku Klux Klan to put a race back under slavery was very disconcerting and almost unreal, but this was also unnatural to what human behavior should be.

According to Matthew: 23:8: *"But be not ye called Rabbi: for one is your Master, even Christ: and all ye are brethren."* If all men are brethren, why would one brother put another under slavery? Only God has the preeminence over the whole of a race or man to do as He will; to confirm or deny rights and movements or actions. *Master Study Bible, King James Version, 2001*

One race's intolerance of another can be compared to the beast of the field or a pride of Lions. Prides of Lions are kept pure, no tolerance for others to come in. This will cause extinction of that pride. So it is with man! Schultz (2008) noted that, "God's toleration of injustice has a purpose. It is to show men that they are like the animals. The presence of injustice in the world and the fact of human mortality demonstrate that we are like beast. Perhaps in our injustice, we sink to a level below the beast (Elwell, Baker's Commentary on the Bible, P440).

Wilson (1978) said on human aggression that, "Human beings are strongly predisposed to respond with unreasoning hatred to external threats and to escalate their hostility sufficiently to overwhelm the source of the threat by a respectably wide margin of safety. Our brains do appear to be programmed to the following extent that we are inclined to partition other people into friends and aliens, in the same sense that birds are inclined to learn territorial songs and to navigate by the polar constellations. We tend to fear deeply the actions of strangers and to solve conflict by aggression. We can only work our way around them. To let them rest latent and un-summoned we must consciously undertake those difficulty and rarely travelled pathways in psychological development that lead to mastery over and reduction of the profound human tendency to violence", p119.

Trying to oppress the black race in slavery no matter the type, is a transience act, it will not last, as history reminds us. Endemic to this organization was the parasitic feeding off hate that the Ku Klux Klan indulged in.

F R E E D O M
V I I I I I I

"There are no shortcuts to any place worth going"
—Beverly Sills

Thus, freedom is a waterfall of possibilities. Sometimes that freedom like the waterfall has to run over rocks and like the power of water, freedom, cannot be stopped or restrained very long. The stream follows on a predestined, circumstantial and set path. Therefore, freedom, like the water that run over rocks; there are no shortcuts for the minority races it was time-labored process. The time-labored process that bought freedom, for the Negro, was build using one board and one nail of the law at a time. The sanction for man to be free came through The Constitution of the United States. *United States Constitution, 1776*

As life and circumstances, kicked the Negro around, equal rights and freedom seemed to get farther and farther away. Freedom is like soaring on eagles wings observing as one go all of the joys of life that free freedom can offer.

To take away the ability of an eagle to soar, an act of crippling its wings, prevents him from flying and enjoying the freedom and joys that life has to offers. The Negro was that eagle with a crippled wing, which need healing. Here, the Negro suffered an abject poverty of spirit along this liquid, rugged and rocky path to freedom.

So then, when there is no wing room, eagles cannot exercise that freedom of flight. An Eagles wings are eight feet from tip to tip. When an eagle is injured, it keep its soaring tools by it side, which shows an abject poverty of spirit. That abject poverty of spirit can apply to the Negro as well.

The Negro like the eagle, lost their will to soar, because of the many wounds inflicted. There was no soaring room for the Negro race, no room to exercise their freedom, not of flight like the eagle, but to live in peace and safety like any humans would expect and that The Constitution of the United States guaranteed. They, like the eagle, kept their soaring tools close to their side. The eagle's wings can be repaired which allowing healing, so the spirit of the Negro was repaired to allow healing by the Civil Rights Movement.

There was no quality of mercy with the Ku Klux Klan for other races of people, no matter who they were, it just so happened that the Negro race was convenient and an easy target, just as Haman of old targeted the Jews because of hate. Hate is a terrible odious feeling, and when manifested through actions against another human or race, of people those actions should be abhorrent to the onlookers.

The Ku Klux Klan acted without showing any mercy toward the Negro race and their helpers. The Klan was a one-act play, written with one focus making the Negro race suffer, wherefore ridding the world of blacks became an addiction. The Ku Klux Klan were saboteurs of freedom, they were like parasites upon the black race, making their lives miserable and almost unbearable.

QUOTES

"The quality of mercy is not strained; it falls like a gentle rain from Heaven."
—William Shakespeare

"These were the best of times; these were the worst of times."
—Charles Dickens

"Memories are like the Mississippi River:
altered by man but always remembering its true path."
—Toni Morrison

I Lived On the Other Side of the Line
The Civil Rights Era Through The Eyes Of A Child: The Road To Freedom
1960's-1970's Turbulent Years and Where Are We Now?
Memoirs of Shane Elizabeth Washington

CHAPTER 1

Faith has seen many generation of people and races of people through hard times, floods, wars, dissonance, unrest, and fights for freedom. Faith is one of the foundations upon which this Country, The United States of America was built. As stated in Hebrews 11:1 Faith is the substance of things hoped for and the evidence of thing not seen, *Master Bible King James Version, 2001.*

We all have faith in something, but this kind or type of faith is in God, the maker of all Mankind. These types of faith and hope were also, written into The Constitution of the United States. We all live under these faiths and hopes of freedom, equality and justice for all in the United States.

The Forefathers built this country based on faith and hope for a better nation, a new nation where there was no slavery and freedom of religion. At one time, in the lives of the immigrants from England, they were slaves to the religious nation that the Church of England, ruled by the King, which was the religion of choice for all men. The notion that England had of no religious freedom was rejected and fought, against by the Pilgrims. They left England to look for a newer and better world, where all men would be free to make a choice; be they bad choices or good choices. Without faith and hope, this nation would not be standing today. There is a saying that "history repeats itself." The people came to America and adopted a "copycat" mentality. *http://www.richmondancestry.org/pilgrim.shtml*

Knowingly, the Forefathers allowed the idea of slavery be written into the Constitution and stay in the Constitution of the United States. This act of ignoring this fact was a testimony to their "agreement" with the idea of slavery. Was it to keep the states unified or keep the Border States from succeeding?

The Border States during the Civil War were: Maryland, Delaware, Kentucky, and Missouri. *http://www.civilwarhome.com/borderstates.htm*

Therefore, when the 15th Amendment was written for equal rights for all men this "all" was never intended to include the black race. Buying and selling man's freedom for the price of states being loyal to the North is poor reasoning.

As a rule, freedom, Justice and equality for each and every one is a *Free Rider*, which does not limit the other person from enjoying the same privilege, so why deny a right that comes, first from the Constitution; secondly, from the fact that a person or race of people is on American soil. *Essentials of Economics Schiller, Free Rider Dilemma, p191*

We all own a piece of the soil which these rights to freedom, for all is the idea upon which, America the new nation was built. However, freedom was not easy to come by. These freedoms were fought for before and after the founding , of America. Everyone contributed in the same way to that freedom. If denial or freedom is the "rule of the day" as it was for so long for the black man, why not deny it for everyone. Only God can decide who can be free or who cannot be free. He did not make man to be slaves to other men. As that famous line in the Movie the Ten Commandments made by John Derek (1926-1998) "God made men, men made slaves." Power is a danger in the wrong hands.

In contrast, the want for power destroyed Satan. His superego gratification gave him a need to be powerful on Earth and in Heaven. He swept up to Heaven to take over and found it was a self-destructive effort Revelations 12:9: And the great dragon was cast out, that old serpent, called the Devil and Satan, which deceiveth the whole world: he was cast out into the earth and his angels were cast out with him. In the same framework of logic, a want for power over other men ends with the same results; man trying to enslave man is self-destructive, *Master Study Bible King James Version, 2001*.

Christ said, "I saw Satan fall from Heaven like lightening, Revelations 16: Lighting is an instantaneous action; man can rise and fall in the same manner, Master Study Bible King James Version, 200.

We all look for our El Dorado in life. Riches can come in all shapes and forms. Power was the riches sought by the Ku Klux Klan. Power was their El Dorado, power over another race of people. Living in a fearful condition, so fenced in by fear can be compared to a "Hell's Outhouse" all the dredge of life was there for the black race. The Ku Klux Klan's "Hell's Outhouse" that one organization, made life on earth, for a while, for the black race, was a fiery hell.

The "We" in the Constitution had a unity. That unity was based on, one of the three principles of structure: Unity of Time, Unity of Place, and Unity of Action, a whole of totality as combining all the parts into one, www.definition. com. October 12, 2012

The Forefathers had an oneness in mind as they gathered to pin and approve the Constitution. They were in accord, harmonious and in agreement as how to unify and build a strong nation of people. An act of combining all the people, of America into one to make a whole is embodied the Document written by the Forefathers of America, The Constitution of the United States. The signatures on the Constitution authenticated by our Forefathers and showed that they were in agreement with what was in the written document. On the other hand, it appeared the Forefathers of this nation were united only in the words that were written in Constitution and not in reality.

There was no rights, for the black race, that is, no real right, just paper right, which as Former President of South Africa Nelson Mandela said, "Can man make a man less than what he is capable of being." In this sense, humans need to be a version of themselves and not what man design for them looks like. "Always, be a first-rate version of yourself, instead of a second-rate version of somebody else, *Judy Garland*." In this sense, looking in that mirror of self, one would want to see an image, of self, created by self, and not live like a shadow in a version of someone else. We each are individuals and should live that way.

Moreover, how do you go about justifying the reason for putting man in to the same kind of slavery they just freed themselves from, an ideology that one race of people should server another and become beast of burdens. This ideology had tentacles like an Octopus. Those tentacles would spread out and catch and squeezed the life out of another race of human beings. An Octopus has a head with two eyes, but no body, and no heart, man has to have a body to have a heart.

The ideology, like the tentacles, sucked people in and created a monster that spread itself all over the South. Only faith and hope would eventually defeat this monster. The 1960's saw this ideology take hold and grow into a fever that medicine could not cure, not at that time anyway. Hence, enslavement whether by an idea or chains carries the same results, freedom is forfeited.

Ordinarily, we should learn from history. The Jews were enslaved in Egypt because of their greatness in number. The Egyptians put them in chains because of an ideology. Blacks begin to be a greatest in number. Men always fear what they do not understand. Fear has a debilitating affect upon man's mind. Also, from this perspective, fear can be used as an excuse to hurt and destroy for what is in already our hearts. Here's that Octopus head analogy again.

According to the book of *Genesis 45:18: And take you father and your households, and come unto me: and I will give you the good of the land of Egypt, and ye shall eat the fat of the land. Master Study Bible, King James Version, 2001*

Israel went down to Egypt to prosper, to do well, to be near Joseph, Jacobs's son that was sold into slavery 20 years before by his brethren.

All men are brethren, therefore why can one have the heart to put the other into slavery whether by chains or ideology?

Matthew 23:8. But you, do not be called 'Rabbi'; for One is your Teacher, the Christ, and you are all brethren. *Master Study Bible, King James Version, 2001*

The Pharaoh, at that time, had Joseph second in command with no one higher. According to Genesis 41:38, 40, "And Pharaoh said unto his servants, "Can we find such a one as this, a man in whom the Spirit of God is. Thou shall be over my house, and according unto they word shall all my people be ruled; only in the throne will I be greater than thou." However, when Pharaoh and Joseph were no longer alive, the new Pharaoh was encouraged to put the Jews in bondage because they were greater in number than the Egyptians, therefore, bondage for the Jews started and lasted for more than four hundred years. *Master Study Bible, King James Version, 2001.*

Does this sound familiar?

In comparison, slaves were also, shipped from Africa to America; as such, slavery lasted for more than 400 years. According to Bristol (2013), "There are no complete records and estimates vary from a few millions to 100,000,000 people. Most historians today think that, according to the shipping records available, between 9 and 11 million people were taken out of Africa by European slave traders and landed alive on the other side of the Atlantic." http://discoveringbristol.org.uk/slavery/routes/from-africa-to-america/atlantic-crossing/people-taken-from-africa/

In this sense, humans keep repeating themselves, in history. Do we as humans ever learn? According to Teamoh, et.al (1990) God made man, man make slaves, p 103-108.

Slavery was a terrible and degrading thing in antiquity, as in any age. God alone is the creator and owner of all that exist, especially human beings.

That traffic should be made of human beings is unconscionable in His sight. In this regard, Rome reached the limits of degradation. Such arrogance cried out for judgment and the wrath of God was poured out in double measure: Revelations 18:6, "Reward her even as she rewarded you, and double unto her double according to her works: in this cup which she filled fill to her double." *Master Study Bible, King James Version, 2001*

The Lamentation continues with an elaboration of Rome's great wealth and luxury and a second observation that she dashed from the heights of power to the rubble of destructions in the blink of an eye, Revelation 18:13,16,17 (Baker's Commentary, Walter A. Elwell).

When our Forefathers left England, they lived on the other side of the lines. How soon we forget when freedom comes and we can make our own choices. Choice should be freedom for everyone, every race, every creed, not freedom for some and not for others.

Childhood memories, like photos of still life, it is etched in time – unchanging; they cannot be altered. As such, so are the memories of a childhood. Wherefore, during that childhood a child's memory is like putty clay in the hands of a potter. The potter shapes the clay again and again at their will. The clay, like a child's memory is fragile it can be crumbled and torn apart like a piece of tissue.

Therefore, the potter has to handle with care that piece of clay; therefore, humans have to handle with care that conscious of a child. That child's memory like that piece of clay is subject to the potters will to shape and mold. Molding a child can have an everlasting effect on his life and the way they think and their perceptions of life. Unlike clay, if the potter does not shape that piece of clay just right it can be re-shaped again. Unlike a child's memory, damage done to the clay is not permanent. Unfortunately, a child's memory like a photograph of still-life, cannot be reshaped as you would a piece of clay putty, the damage that is done can be permanently.

Children draw lines in the sand when they play hopscotch, marbles or have foot races, but these lines do not restrict human freedom. Lines of this kind are there only for that period, of time until that game is played or at least, until a winner is declared. Lines separate each state of this great country and define territories; these are boundaries so that, the laws and the constitutional rights of citizens can be honored.

In this light, each state makes their laws that are applicable to that area. These types of lines are for the good of all people. Lines should not separate and divide rights of a race of people or set territories lines that a races of people should not crossed on to. The Constitutional lines were drawn for each human beings to have free rights to the freedoms guaranteed them.

There are certain lines that can-be-drawn by man that are, for the benefit of all. But, if the lines that are drawn is to restrict one race or segment of people to certain area, parts of a city where they can and cannot shop or what water fountain they may drink from, it cannot be counted as a whole nation; rights for some and not for others. Water is a natural resource free to all, and when one man tries to limit the other access to this freedom then man has gone too far and labeled himself an equal to God Almighty. God drew lines, whether they were mental or physical for humans, which are his right, because he is God, the maker of all men.

Therefore, restricting human freedom is not a privilege given to any man, woman, or child no matter the race, creed, color, or natural origin. The Pharaohs of old in Egypt delegated themselves this right and authority, the Emperors of Rome; the Caesar families called themselves Gods and took this right. Both of these powers drew lines in the sand whether mental or physical, they are nonetheless lines. Conquers of the world, fighting machines could be assigned to both the powers of Egypt and Rome. *patachu.com/egypt-ancient-roman-conquest-and-occupation-historic*

The Emancipation Proclamation (1862) came in on the hills of the Constitution and restated those rights that were already on the books, as if were, for all citizens. Lincoln did not see the Negro race as "property", but as worthwhile members of this great nation and deserved the right to enjoy those freedoms that the Constitution stated that all citizens were entitled to.

CHAPTER 2

The Emancipation Proclamation was a breath of fresh air pumped into a southern society with the citizens living in a culture shrouded in bias and race.

Even though sectional conflicts over slavery had been a major cause of the war, ending Slavery was not a goal of the war. President Abraham Lincoln signed the first Emancipation Proclamation on September 22, 1862, stating that, "Slaves in those states or part of state still in rebellion as of January 1, 1863, would be declared free." One hundred days later, with the rebellion unabated, President Lincoln issued the final Emancipation Proclamation on January 1, 1863 announcing, "that all persons held as slaves" within the rebellious areas "are and henceforward shall be free."

Initially, the war between the North and South was fought by the North to prevent the secession of the southern states and preserve the union. Lincoln's bold step to change the goals of the war was a military measure and came just a few days after the Union's victory in the Battle of Antietam. The Army of the Potomac, under the command of George McClellan, mounted a series of powerful assaults against Robert E. Lee's forces near Sharpsburg, Maryland, on September 17, 1862. *http://www.civilwar.org/battlefields/antietam.html*

With the proclamation, he hoped to inspire blacks and slaves in the Confederacy in particular, to support Union cause and keep England and France from giving political recognition and military aid to the Confederacy. Because of the military measure, however, the Emancipation Proclamation was limited in many ways. It applied only to states that had seceded from the Union, leaving slavery untouched in the loyal Border States. It also exempted parts of the Confederacy that had come under Union control. Most important, the freedom it promised depended upon Union military victory.

Blacks agreeing to join the battle for freedom and keep the incumbencies of political chains from tighten even more by England and France given military recognition and military aid to the confederacy, were a key component in the Civil War and the battle for the "united" states. From the first day of the Civil War, slaves acted to secure their own liberty.

The Emancipation Proclamation confirmed their insistence that the war for the Union must become a war for freedom. The presence of the now freed slaves, added a moral force to the union cause; thereby, strengthening the union militarily and politically.

This was a breakthrough on the road to finally ending slavery.

http//www.ourdocuments.gov.php?flash=true&doc=34, October 17, 2012

Slavery for its intents and purposes was gone according to the Emancipation Proclamation; it was gone on paper but not gone in actuality. Some of the physical slavery was gone. In this case, the physical slavery was replaced by another kind of slavery; an emotional one. The first slavery was a physical one under the master's whip; however, the second type of slavery that showed its head was one of an emotional or mental dispensation. However, the Negro saw a stagflation of their freedom, equal right and justice rights that were endorsed, twice by President Abraham Lincoln.

Besides, the emotional and mental types of slaveries were main focus was on putting fear, dread and emotional stress in the minds of a race of people. Even though this fear, dread and emotional stress affected people across the South of all races; for the most part, the black race was the ones that mainly felt the effects. Change has always been hard for humans no matter the continent you live on.

Wherefore, hate is a by-product of change. Humans hate to leave what we know as the status quo in life for a more progressive or improved ideology. Ideology in this sense is not a threat to humanity, because of the necessity for change. In fact, The Constitution of the Unites States gave all men equal right and equal freedom. People of color and the black members of the human race, were not intended to be beasts of burden. God make animals for this task. We do not chain our animals or make them slaves, so why do we chain and make slaves of other humans? Human beings are all the same, they are flesh and blood entitled to freedom and the pursuit of happiness.

No one, like to be told, what he or she can and cannot do in life. Moreover, it is put on another level when, humans put other humans in chains, whether they are mental, physical or emotional chains. The Preamble to The Constitution states that: "We the people of the Unites States in order to form a more perfect union." *Preamble to the Constitution of the United States, 1786 http://www.usconstitution.net/const.html*

That perfect union includes blacks, whites, Native Americans and all other nationalities and races that are citizens of this great country.

CHAPTER 3

Manifest Destiny, according to the encyclopedia, was a belief extensively held by Americans in the 19th century that the United States was destined to expand across the continent. This concept, born out of "A sense of mission to redeem the Old World by extraordinary example…generated by the possibility of a new earth for building a new heaven." This doctrine and attitude provided fertile ground to expand as far as they wanted. The Manifest Destiny always limped along because of internal constraints and the soaring issue of slavery, which never became a national priority. *www.encyclopedia.com, November 21, 2012*

One of the proponents of the Manifest Destiny, John Adams in 1843, changed his mind about the dogma and rejected the doctrine, because it meant the expansion of slavery in Texas. *www.history.com/topics/manifest-destiny December 25, 2012*

The Ku Klux Klan "treated" themselves to the self-appointed duty of getting rid of the black race, introduced a Manifest Destiny, of their own creation. The Ku Klux Klan was like a barn fire with coal oil poured over it waiting for the match to light the fire. The Civil Rights Movement was that match.

Manifest Destiny was a product of the nineteenth century an imperialistic view that America was destined to expand across the North American Continent.

The Manifest Destiny in reference to the Ku Klux Klan was an aberration supported by this semi-small group in the South. They were aggressive in their effort to expand the propaganda they spread through fear and hate. This expansion blossomed into the shot lived age of the Ku Klux Klan to the 1960. *Manifest Destiny, about.com, November 26, 2012*

The Ku Klux Klan had defined core values. The Ku Klux Klan were Absolutists. Absolutism is defined as, a political system in which the power of a ruler is unchecked. The Ku Klux Klan's power went unchecked, for it seemed like an eternity before any action were taken, to control this group. The Ku Klux Klan's devotion was to supremacy and preservation of the white race.

However, there was one fact that seemed to escape the Klan. Japheth, the father of the white race was also a brother of Ham, the father of the black race and Shem the father of the Jewish race. The second fact that they seemed to overlook was that, all three were of one blood and one father. And God blessed Noah and his sons, and said unto them, *"Be fruitful and multiply and replenish the earth"*, Genesis 9:1.

They spoke of American Indians as savages, the Indians lost everything that belong to them by being put on reservations and run into hills and swamps of a land they inhabited first. Shane said her parents told she and her siblings that the Ku Klux Klan said about the Native Americans that, "They got what was coming to them was the comment."

Unfortunately, fellow African Countrymen were also the reason for slavery. Africans were selling each other. Furthermore, America was founded by people who were Christians with their freedoms being based on Christian principles whom the Ku Klux Klan claimed connections. *http//www.cail.org.all/Mischb/davkk.htm*

Likewise, these kinds of thoughts and fallacies led adherents to their convictions and practice of this ideology. Their reasoning was warped and viewpoints skewed to fit their own thoughts and practices. The Ku Klux Klan was an imperialistic white supremacy group with ideals and visions of grandeur.

With the centuries of hate or the Hamanistic ideology looming like a thick cloud over their members, the Ku Klux Klan acted as a vanguard in their punishment factor for the black race because the race was different. Their ideas were antediluvian and a historical interspersion like, Haman of old.

The name Haman means, magnificent or supreme as the Ku Klux Klan thought they were magnificently supreme beings over every other race, except their own color, and even their supremacy extended to their own race, if their loyalty did not seem to mirror the Ku Klux Klan's. In this wise, Haman could be seen as the Father of Totalitarianism; he had no respect for, but rather contempt for any moral or legal restraints, which was written to protect the vulnerable from tyranny. *Baker Commentary on The Bible, Elwell, Walter, p.327*

The Ku Klux Klan carried out their Manifest Destiny of expansion even more so from the early 1950-1970's, actively and aggressively, like venom from a rattlesnake, the Klan poisoned everything and everybody they touched.

There are always intervening factors in both the cases of the intended extermination or annihilation of a race.

Esther was an intervening factor for the Jews in Persia. Mordecai said, "For if though altogether holdest thy peace at this time, then shall their enlargement and deliverance arise to the Jews from another place; but thou and they father's house shall be destroyed: and who knoweth whether thou art come to the kingdom for such as time as this?" Esther 4:14. *Master Study Bible, King James Version, 2001.*

Heroes like Martin Luther King, Jr., Lyndon Baines Johnson, John F. Kennedy, Jr., Moses, Deborah, Joshua, and finally our Lord Jesus Christ, were all intervening factors for the Back race, Native American, Jews, Arabs, and any other race that lived in America or every other nation that was not white or the race of choice at that time. The ideas and schemes of the Ku Klux Klan were un-masked and hung on the gallows of this County's "We've had enough."

The Ku Klux Klan perpetrated violence that insinuated itself upon the South in the 1960's. They took the opportunity during the Civil Rights Era in the 1960's to carry out its beliefs and culture upon one race of people, the black race. The Ku Klux Klan was the perpetrators of this kind of mental and physical violence. Other races were subject to their colorful arrays of violence, if they thought that you would assist the black race or disagree with the Ku Klux Klan's ideology about blacks.

The Ku Klux Klan was bullies during that time just as many people live with the bullies of the world now. Their ideology was a mental discourse that resulted in a physical determent to those targeted.

The Ku Klux Klan objectified and trivialized the black race. They did not see the Negro race as humans, but objects that could be used, told what to do, kicked around, and pushed to the side if their presence wasn't convenient, which in their minds were never. They were a belittled people with no significance in the eyes of the Ku Klux Klan.

The Ku Klux Klan had not come to the realization that freedom and equality were already facts for the black race. These freedoms are already in place for all humans and these two rights can never be divorced. God is the Father of all and Jesus is Lord. Therefore, if specificity is needed, as far as, the earthly part is concerned, The United States Constitution and the Emancipation Proclamation was law; and rights and freedom were already there for the black race to participate in this society as free men and live in peace without fear and assault.

American society is like a well-sewn quilt, sewn together to make one large quilt. There can be no pieces left out, which includes the black race as well.

Shane said, "Comparing the Klan to the Dons of Old California, like the Dons, who served the Governor, of Old California, extracting all of the people's money through taxes, which added heavy burdens upon them and took away their joy and peace of mind. In the same way, the Ku Klux Klan, extracted peace, justice, joy and freedom from the black race through the imposition of fear, which were like heavy chains and the extractions of these freedoms was like levying heavy taxes that became heavy burdens on the black race."

Those heavy burdens were the chains of slavery; they, still existed though, they were mental chains of slavery, but nonetheless, still chains. Chains binds, prevent freedom of thought, chains keep you in one place or one position, chains renders you unable to have the freedom to move about. The chains of fear are the worse kind; they are debilitating and binding. There is no freedom in fear.

Hence, remaining in a position of status quo is any society is deadly. People must embrace the future, change and grow in society. Individual and groups must embrace differences; different races, cultures, and ideas. There was an apparent "disconnect" in our society that had gone unnoticed and unchecked for generations with the one race bearing the brunt, of this disconnect.

The Ku Klux Klan held the black race hostage through fear. Fear became a "chronic condition" initiated by a minority group in the South that operated on hate and bias because of the difference and an attitude of supremacy. How can you fight back if you are afraid for your life or your family's life?

With the mentality of fear spreading, the Ku Klux Klan pulled that pool of thought to the center of the life of people across the South. The black race did not deserve rights, freedoms, and peace of mind to become a true part of that "We" the people of the United States. The unified states became a reality, but not a unified people. There was still a disconnection with the united people part of the Preamble to the Constitution.

There was a genesis of a race and a genesis of an idea during the nineteen sixties and the Civil Rights Movement. Before the Civil Rights Movement when there were positive steps taken to level the playing field, the black race had a watered down diluted version of equality, justice, fairness, and peace of mind.

Those rights depended on which part of the United States you resided in, if it was the Southern part, the black populous felt it more acutely.

The justice that was handed out to the Negro had a razor sharp-edge that cut and caused pain and suffering both emotionally, mentally, physically, and socially. Diluted justice is distasteful as is diluted coffee, no flavor and no richness to it. Justice cannot be handled as if it is A La Cart' a meal, set in buffet style to chosen from picking what you want and leaving the rest, with justice and equality it is all or none.

A La Carte' justice is not justice. Some of this, that and the other is no way for any race or individual to live. You can be free, but here are the conditions. Justice, equality and freedom are unified rights, either you are free or you are not.

So then, these freedoms are not a Classical Viewpoint as John Keys (1936) said about the American economy that, "Calamity would recur if we relied on the market mechanism to self-adjust." The American Economy is not self-adjusting nor are freedom rights self-adjusting with both ideas action has to be made to move the child along to maturity or at the minimum, productivity; some action has to be taken or intervention has to be done to ensure success. Essentials of Economics, *Keys, pp.33-34*

Martin Luther King, Jr., was the intervening factor in the 1960s facilitated by that one action of a citizen refusing to give up her seat on a bus in Montgomery, Alabama. This A La Carte' freedom had gone on far too long. Martin Luther King, Jr. was a helper, when man has troubles; we always look for the helpers.

This mentality of race and justice that the Klan used was like a train off the main track. Taking a sidetrack away from the main track takes the train in a different direction. That train that was side-tracked would be sent a "long way" around until it meets again with the train that runs on the main track. As a result, justice was side-tracked for the black race, for miles down the track, which turned into year, hundreds of years until a semblance of true justice was finally realized.

Above all, "Success isn't a result of spontaneous combustion. You must set yourself on fire, *Arnold H. Glasow.*" *www.goodreads.com/author/quotes/1965567.*

The Civil Rights Movement was the fire that helped the Negro finally, fight back. The fires to fight-back, were built by the Civil Rights Movement; dare we say that these fires cannot be put out.

The Civil Rights Movement of the 1960s was the first mile of the new track for the train of justice to run on. Sometimes it takes firing the old engineers and hiring new ones. Martin Luther King, Jr., was the new engineer that put that side-traced train back on the track of justice, for the black or underdog race.

Accordingly, the war, for freedom was fought with the loaded gun of fairness and not with sticks that break which has no power. Wars are always two opposing forces. One side cannot fight a war without some other force opposing it. Ideology and racist mentality was one of the many opposing forces. The Ku Klux Klan another opposing force, fear another opposing force, especially of what we do not understand about another race or culture.

Freedom was, for 400 years plus, a stolen American dream, for the Negro race. Their freedom was heist by a mentality of a Feudal type system of class and importance.

A Feudal System is in antiquity and in modern times; in the Marxist usage it refers to a type of society and economy characterized by serfdom, generally succeeding the economic systems based on slavery and preceding capitalism. The word from the Germanic *fehu-od*(from which is derived the English and French *fief*)— that is, "property in cattle" and, later, "tenure" or "property in land"- stresses the importance, in the system, of land tenure and the rights and privileges attached to it. Since the seventeenth century, the complex of tenurial and personal relationships and economic, social, and political dependencies that centered on the fief have increasingly been regarded as a scaffold of social stratification and political organization. *http://www.encyclopedia.com/topic/feudalism.aspx*

Like stitches sewn into fine tapestry, freedom was a tapestry sewn into Constitution of the United States, for justice and equality, for all of humans regardless of race, creed or color. It is said that, "History repeats itself." This is a true statement. In fact, there has never been a truer statement made. History does repeat itself, in this sense, should history repeat itself? In the History, of the United States of America, this statement have been found to be true, too many times.

So many things repeat themselves in this country. Therefore, there are things that should never repeat themselves as such are: the lack of freedom, the lack of justice, the lack of liberty and the lack equality. This cause-effect type of situation presented itself at an inconvenient time in America. The push for freedom was a train on the main track, no more sidetrack for the rights of all people including the black race and any others. The Rights of Passage (important transitional periods in a person's life) had been discovered; there would be no turning back. On the other hand, "Lack" initiated by violence always causes mental pain. These Rights, of Passage, cannot be denied a free people. Those Rights of Passage were given to the Negro by their freedom, as citizens of America. *http://dictionary. reference.com/browse/rites+of+passage*

Mental violence is worse than any other act of violence. Mental violence is like fear laced with arsenic, it is deadly. Fear kills, fear stalemates, and fear can make you even harm self. This is what the act of bullying will do. This was one of the many weapons used by the Ku Klux Klan. Bullying is always a group-project. No one person was brave enough, on their own, to carry out any single act against a person. Had any Ku Klux Klan member been alone would not have approached one of the blacks in the community. They knew they would have a battle on their hands. They simply were not brave enough to try any physical violence as a lone rider.

Consequently, this type of mentality can create Falsidical Paradoxes'. Namely, the logic of this mentality requires a stretch.

CHAPTER 4

The Ku Klux Klan lived in a Falsidical Paradox. A Falsidical Paradox is a valid, logical demonstration of absurdities, ideologies, or philosophies. A Paradox is a passion of thought. However, the ultimate potentiation of every passion is always to will its own downfall, and so the ultimate passion of the understanding to will the collision, although in one way or another, the collision must become its downfall, Soren Kierkegaard------. This then is the ultimate paradox of thought to want to discover something that "thought" cannot think (Lazio, Heraclites, Meister, Eckhart, Hegel, Kierkegaard and Nietzsche). Date

The Ku Klux Klan developed the passion to rid the world of the black race. The Ku Klux Klan's notion to get rid of the black race and deny them freedom or equal-rights, was a self-refuting (false) idea. These types of ideas are akin to dictatorial minds like those of Hitler, Stalin, Nero, Caesar, and etc. *www. wikipedia.org/wik/self-refutingl-idea.*

How do you eliminate a race of people successfully; it has been tried since the beginning of time. The Ku Klux Klan's idea to annihilate the black race became self-consuming. This is an unthinkable thought, a false paradox. It was logical to them, but when the thought became a test field, it failed. History tells us of the failure of these types of philosophies is held up as a banner for success; i.e. the Fall of Rome, and the fall of Babylon, two great empires, both self-refuting dictatorially led by mad men.

The idea to eliminate the black race eventually destroyed the Klan. Their ideas were rejected by logical minds; the people of America. The Ku Klux Klan were Terrorists, there is no other term or name for a group with ideologies of this kind. The Ku Klux Klan put this ideology to test of eliminating the black race was in a small and sporadically populated community, in North Mobile County.

This type of Paradoxical Falsity mentality was attempted by one, of the citizens of the white community called, Red.

CHAPTER 5

Shane said that "Georgetown was sporadically populated; therefore, it made it much easier for the families to be targeted by this evil monster. The families were spread-out and not very close together; being vigilant was wise for each household to keep themselves and each other safe."

Shane continued to say that, "On the other hand, Chunchula had a very centralized community of blacks that lived on a strip of Georgetown Road starting where the Community Baptist Church stands. The community ran all the way to Highway 45 on both sides of the road and down in two more communities called the bottom or Boggy Branch and Gravel Hill. Now, the bottom was like a gated community, not as we know gated today, but by virtue of the road which was one way in and one way out. The other way was through a swamp like area, far too dangerous to try to get across. The people were more secure because of the swampland that surrounded the community. One would need to familiar with the bottom before taking a chance of going into that community. There were two ways in and two ways out; it was either the swamp or the road."

"Without knowing where you are, was a trap in-and-of-itself. I guess you could disappear if you were not careful or if you were not a regular member of the community. There were no white people living in the "bottom." Shane said, "She could not ever remember even hear telling of any white's that went in the bottom; no electricity, no paved roads, not even an insurance man went in if they weren't black." Bravery wasn't a forte" of the Ku Klux Klan not if they were in a single number. They went by the old adage, "Safety in numbers."

Shane told me that she knew that this was true. Because, one of the members of the white community called "Red", drove up in their yard one day and got out-of his truck and approached her father William while he was standing near the corn crib and said, "Hey boy." William didn't say anything, he just continued to stand with the pitch fork in his hand that he was piling corn in their crib with. Red said again, "Did you hear me boy?" Answer me nigger, did you hear me? Shane's commented that her father William said in a very calm voice, "*If you name your big toe nigger, you'll have one of your own, my name is Mr. Washington when you get the time.* There is nothing for you here, so why are you in my yard? Shane said, "Red just stood there for a second, seemingly not knowing what to say. He looked around to see who else might be behind him, and all of the Washington children had gathered in a semi-circle behind him. He did not expect, I am sure, to meet this type of bravery."

Thus, during that time, the word "Boy" was a put-down, a racial slur. It equates to the same as calling a black female "Gal." Shane said, "At that moment, Red was in more danger than he realized. William Washington, Jr. was not a man that you could push too far. When he said something, he would back it up. He would not back-down. Red was on private property, as well as, in a total black neighborhood, at that time, and without his regular backup team."

"When this fact became apparent to Red, he began to back-up slowly. He kept backing up, all the while, reaching behind him feeling for his truck, he finally touched it. A nervous and scared sigh of relief came from his already parted lips; which, Shane said, "She heard across the yard where she was standing quietly watching the scene unfold." Fumbling for a while, Red finally very clumsily opened the truck door got in and began desperately groping for his key. The look of Red's face became increasingly a flushed pink color while he looked for his keys. He would look up and then down again repeatedly until he found the right key. He fumbled and floundered seemingly forever looking for those keys. He finally found them!"

"Red nervously started his truck, backed-up as quickly as his vehicle would move in its condition and turned the truck towards the highway. He sped away as if something or someone was chasing him. Shane expressed to me that, "From where she stood and from the red blushes on his face, anyone could see the expressions he had on his face that looked like it said, "Maybe this wasn't a good idea after all under any circumstances; now, how do I get myself out of this tight spot? Run! Run!"

"Apparently, Red saw what everyone knew, which was that, William Washington, Jr. told them, "If you try to hurt or threaten one of my children or my wife, I am coming for somebody, I don't care who it is, but somebody gonna get payback." He meant it. Shane had seen her father and grandfather in action before, neither of them would backup, but just so far. They tried to avoid a fight or confrontation, but if you wanted to press the issue, they could and would accommodate you."

His family was everything to him and no one would molest, bully, or intimidate them without some repercussions. Shane said, "Red, never got nerve enough to come to my father's yard ever again; but, when he was with Tank and his brother Jessie, he was as bad a dude as they come, he thought. If spouting racial slurs made him bad, he had it; but, he was always with his back-up when he spat ugliness out of his mouth."

There seemed to be no sensitivity, of kindness or understanding of the plight of the Negro, nor was there any care. In particular, can two races with two different cultures put away their differences and respect each other, regardless, of their differences? Why must or do man fear what they do not understand or why hate someone because of their skin color?

According to Acts: 17:26: *And hath made of one blood all nations of men for to dwell on all the face of the earth, and hat determined the times before appointed, and the bounds of their habitation.*

CHAPTER 6

The Constitution of the United States is a live document, not one that is collecting dust on a shelf. When the American Revolution was fought it sent a message; that message sent was one, of hope. Gone, were those British shackles that oppressed America for so long. Through the America's Revolution into an American evolution, those shackles of slavery were thrown-off.

Freedom is no longer free, it is a constant struggle..."Posterity, you will never know how much it cost the present generation to preserve your freedom. I hope you will make good use of it. If you do not, I shall repent in heaven that ever I took half the pains to preserve it."...John Adams *http://www.theamericanrevolution.org/*

Accordingly, the Thirteenth Amendment of the Constitution of 1865 ended slavery; but there was still no equality there for all races not yet.

The Gettysburg Address written by Abraham Lincoln mirrored the Constitution. "Four Score and Seven Years ago, our Fathers brought forth on this continent a new nation; conceived in liberty, and dedicated to the proposition that all men are created equal." This was not a celebration of a new freedom or new birth, but the Gettysburg address spoke of idea of equality and a democratic government. *http://www.abrahamlincolnonline. org/lincoln/speeches/gettysburg.htm*

The Unites States Constitution, in contrast, sanctioned the subjugation of enslaving blacks. The defeat of the law that aided the enslavement of the black race, for so long a time, was finally defined and written as part of the Constitution of the United States. This address bought about the change to the Constitution. Lawmakers added the Thirteenth, fourteenth and fifteenth amendments.

Thus, the Thirteenth Amendment read: "Neither slavery nor involuntary servitude, except as a punishment, for crime where of the party shall have been duly convicted, shall exist within the Unites States or any place subject to their jurisdiction. *http://www.archives.gov/historical-docs/document.html?*

This meant, all persons born or naturalized in the United States. Therefore, no states can make any law that would abridge the privileges or immunities of any citizen, nor can any state deprive any person of life, liberty or property without due process of law, or deny any person within its jurisdiction the equal protection of the law. However, no one related this to the Ku Klux Klan especially about, the Negro race. So then, their actions were back in the slavery era that pre-dated the Civil War or the Gettysburg Address.

In 1862, the bitter seeds of the Civil War were growing. Mr. Lincoln, two years from the presidency, wrote, "A house divided against itself cannot stand." *http://www.abrahamlincolnonline.org/lincoln/speeches/house.htm* .

President Lincoln emulated what the Bible said, "And if a kingdom be divided against itself, that kingdom cannot stand. And if a house be divided against itself, that house cannot stand, but hath an end. And if Satan rise up against himself, and be divided, he cannot stand, but hath an end, *Mark 3:24-26.*

In the same wise, neither can a people be divided against themselves survive. This can be either a short or long road to destruction, In contrast, this statement could apply to a people, a nation of people, all races, creed and colors cannot survive without having that common-ground and working together to build this nation and now, in the 1960 work together to make this nation even greater. That would take all of the people of all races.

In particular, the dividing factor that kept this from happening was race, and the territory that was labeled the "South." The Civil War brought the nation together, territory wise, but there were still bloody battles going on for freedom.

President Abraham Lincoln, in Springfield, Missouri in 1857, spoke of the rule or standards for all, of rights and of equality; this was eight years before he freed the slaves in 1865. Lincoln wrote, "Through the Declaration of Independence the framers meant to set up a standard for free society. Further that, this standard, should be familiar to all and revered by all, constantly looked to, constantly labored, for and even though never perfectly attained, constantly approximated; and thereby, constantly spreading, and deepening its influence and augmenting the happiness and value of life to all people of all colors everywhere. God endowed all men with the unalienable rights of life, liberty and the pursuit of happiness. It is an inherent right, of all men.

http://www.mrlincolnandfreedom.org/inside.asp?

The scripture tells us there is a woe unto those by who offense come *Matthew 8:17*: *Woe unto the world because of offences! For it must needs be that offences come; but woe to that man by whom the offence come.*

 The South was still divided against itself; because, the people were not in union in thoughts nor actions. It was necessary for another movement, not a war to take place to affect a change to bring this part of the country together. There were still battles in the South for freedom between the now self-appointed Supremacy Group with their use of machination to devise ways to eliminate any freedom that the blacks had, starting with the right to vote, according to the 15th Amendment.

Section 1.

 The right of citizens of the United States to vote shall not be denied or abridged by the United States or by any state on account of race, color, or previous condition of servitude.

 http://www.law.cornell.edu/constitution/amendmentxv

 However, this effort just gave a fertile ground to more hate and racism, for more than a half of a century since the Ku Klux Klan's inception in 1866 in Tennessee. The Fifteenth Amendment that gave Blacks the right to vote was a game changer; it was more than evident to everyone…especially the Ku Klux Klan. *http://www.law.cornell.edu/constitution/amendmentxv*

 Moreover, there were other races and centuries when this the menace of slavery hung heavy over the nations of people, which can be seen in the enslavement of the Jews and Christians.

CHAPTER 7

Jews in Slavery

On the other hand, the Jews and the Christians suffered at the hands of the Romans; they were a nation of terrorist. They spread fear and intimidation everywhere they went. Known fighting machines, the Romans had layers of rulers and managers who controlled the people with fear.

As a result, of this permeating fear, came the loss of control of their own lives, as well as, the fear that they may lose their lives. The Jews and Christians faced the terrible lions of persecution at the hands of the Romans while they used them for sport at the famous games in the Roman Coliseum.

http://www.mariamilani.com/ancient_rome/christian_persecution_Roman_empire.htm

Intolerance was at the root of the persecutions and rein of fear perpetrated upon these people. In contrast, just as the Ku Klux Klan did the blacks in the Deep South, they executed a reign of terror in the black neighborhoods.

Understandably, like the Jews in Roman society, some of the black citizens in the South were not subject to this kind of terror. Why? Because those citizens in Rome like the one that lived in Chunchula stayed out of the way of harm and danger.

As close as Shane could remember, unless they needed supplies, i.e.: staple goods, clothes or shoes they did not venture far from their homes. Like the Jews, who hid in caves and caverns, in dense forests areas to avoid persecution, the black citizens stayed out of the main stream in the black neighborhood, which most times was a good ways down in the woods or off the main highway.

Even the Ku Klux Klan was not brave enough to venture too far off the beaten path, because, danger lurked in the deep woods in the rural areas where blacks lived. The Ku Klux Klan always had a hit and run strategy. When they ventured off the highway-they ran the risk of disappearing. The Ku Klux Klan like the Romans targeted those people that were easily accessible.

We should look not at others faults or race, creed or color, or likes or differences, but should we not embrace them with an attitude of understanding, at least make the attempt? It is better than putting everyone in the same category.

The Klan was diseased with hate, a lack of care, or understanding. They hated the Negro because they were different. Shane asked her mother and father, "How can this be?" They told her as before, "It is borne from ignorance, and they are a group of people that suffered from intolerance." The Ku Klux Klan suffered from the Machiavellian syndrome.

According to the Oxford Dictionary (1626) Machiavellianism (or machiavellian mask) is, the employment of cunning and duplicity in statecraft or in general conduct", deriving from the Italian Renaissance diplomat and writer Niccolò Machiavelli. http://oxforddictionaries.com/us, February 15, 2013.

In today philosophy, the word has a similar use in modern psychology where it describes one of the dark triad personalities, characterized by a duplicitous interpersonal style associated with cynical beliefs and pragmatic morality. *Stanford Encyclopedia of Philosophy*, http://plato.stanford.edu/entries/machiavelli/ September 13, 2005.

The Ku Klux Klan were a polarized group. They used very scheming, artful, crafty, and conniving ways of dealing with what they called the "problem". They used many machinations to bring to fruition, the plot against the people of the black race…with the main point being, elimination.

Even though Montgomery was a hot spot in the quagmire of the Civil Right Movement, the movement that was taking place in rural communities all over the South was one of fear and exhaustion. Exhaustion from mental strain took a toll on citizens of small communities because there was no one to help. William Washington, Jr. told the neighbors in a meeting, "When there is no one to help, we help ourselves. Stand on your principles of right and wrong. We have to protect our families at all cost. There is no choice. We did not go looking for trouble it came to us. Therefore, we need to deal with it."

In the near vicinity to William, Jr.'s house was his brother and sister-in-law Elbert and Lena Washington. Even though Elbert was a good bit older than William, Jr., he was still a tuff O'Bird. He was one that said even less than William, Jr. According to Shane, "He was never one to tuck his tail and run, like William, Jr. and Sr., he would back up to avoid trouble, but only so far."

Shane said, "But, on the other hand, James Washington and his wife Irma also lived in the neighborhood, but a good two to three miles toward the little town of Chunchula. "Now, he was pretty brave", said Shane , but not like her father William, Jr., James had this screaming wife, who was afraid of her own shadow. She even hid in the closet from lighting, so you know she would run from the threat of another human."

Shane said, "Her fear was of such magnitude that she could hardly leave out of her front or back door. She had a bedroom located in the middle of her shotgun house where she forted herself in. Her curtains were always drawn, doors locked, and each window had a stick over it to secure the window so no one could get in that way. Shane said, "She remembered going to her Aunt Irma's house and entering through the front door. After that, it seemed like you traveled through a tomb, such somber darkish gray surrounding overwhelmed you as you walked through this maze. Because of fear, her aunt was forced to live in these conditions."

Like the thick fog of the early morning that hangs without mercy on a hot summer day, so did terror and violence, hang over the Black communities. Targeting a particular race was the focus of the Ku Klux Klan. The fear and terror that the extremist group perpetrated was evident in the entire community.

When the Ku Klux Klan, are juxtaposed, with words like terrorism or vigilantism, it meant fear and dread. These interactive words describe the evil relationship between the Ku Klux Klan and the meaning of fear. They would carry out a campaign of fear. A name can be associated with the total character and nature of the organization. The Ku Klux Klan meaning a clan we know is a group or entity with the same aim. The Ku Klux Klan had a predisposition to violence.

The Ku Klux Klan was a precursor to a more underlying plan of evil to "rid" the world of its undesirable elements. However, size does not denote effectiveness. In relation to the populous of the United State of America, on a whole, the organization was small. On the other hand, their effectiveness came through the institution of fear into minds of the masses of people that were the object of this evil. The more acts of violence committed and the more dogmatic they became, the more aptly trouble followed.

The Ku Klux Klan used evil like an animal prod. When Shane was in her growing years, her father's farm also had green things and plant life growing in addition to the cows, pigs, horses, etc. When William wanted an animal to "gee or haw", he would use that pointy piece of iron he called a prod to get them going in a certain direction. There was no way that the animal could ignore the prod, because it hurt. Naturally, they would move; it was the same with the prod of fear used against the black or minority race.

Using the sharp prod of fear, made them move instinctively, as with any living species, inflicting pain has a moving effect to it. Being stuck with a needle is painful. Multiply this feeling or the size of a needle by one thousand times; it can paint a vivid picture of the pain and suffering experienced by being prodded with the sharp edges of fear.

There are two important points to look at when speaking of evil. Firstly, evil turns upon itself and become self-destructive in the end. Evil, being destructive by nature, it will destroy anything even itself when there is nothing else to destroy. Secondly, notice how evil can be used to accomplish God's purposes. In Revelation 17:17: God's rule stands supreme over all the acts of men and angels.

Even if we intend things to be evil, God can produce good from them. Genesis 50:20: "But as for you he thought evil against me, but God meant it unto good to bring to pass as it is this day to save much people alive; and Romans 8:28: "All things work for the good of those who love God and are called according to his purpose." *The Master Study Bible, King James Version, 2001.*

This should comfort us all.

From behind a frowning providence, God hides a smiling face as William Cowper said, "God is good, his intentions are good, his will and power is good, and his actions are good." Therefore, evil can never stop God's good from being done and in its own peculiar way; evil only cooperates, in the accomplishing of God's good will. *Elwell Bible Commentary, p419*

The decision that the members of the community had to make was to stay on the diving board that afforded them safety, which some of the members of the community did, or jump headlong into the pool that was filled with fear and violence.

The ones that hung back and stayed on the diving board were just stupefied with fear to the point that it engulfed their lives and took away their ability to stand-up for themselves. The bemusement hung so heavy that certain men of the community sweated profusely when the thought of the Ku Klux Klan being an eminent danger in that community, because of the color of their skin. Shane said that, "She thought that if they could have been like a Chameleon; they would have changed their skin. But to what was her question?"

At this time, in the Chunchula/Georgetown communities it was inconvenient and not very appealing to be in the black race. There was safety in other "colors" they thought.

William, Jr. said, "No one should allow an idea or ideology to stupefy them to the point that it made it seem their feet were set in cement, preventing them from being able to move or to think, for that matter." It is like being on a diving board over a swimming pool, afraid to jump.

A diving board over a swimming pool extends out over the pool, which is just as dangerous as being in the pool. The board is not sturdy enough to stand up under too much pressure, but on the other hand, a pool usually has cement bottoms or some other type of solid bottom that can help ground you. Hanging back has never been appealing to William, Jr. and his family.

Both William Jr. and Sr. were always right in the thick of being involved in the community. William, Jr. and William, Sr. and other members of the Washington family took a stand, which would prove to be a divining rod for the community and the other male populous that lived there. "I wouldn't say they were mean, Shane said to me, but you couldn't push them too far."

Even though the Klan had a pugnacious aura about them; they were still humans and did not want the reverse of the bias that they displayed to fall like a cloud over their families, wife or children. This was definitely a possibility. As a result, of this, when humans are pushed far enough they will retaliate in some way. As such, even animals have this type of instinct; they have the need and will to survive, as it was with the black citizens of the Chunchula and Georgetown communities.

William Washington, Jr. meant what he said about coming for somebody, he did not care who it was. Therefore, families in the white neighborhood did not take the chance. Even though they did not bother the Washington family directly, there was still racial bias, racial slurs, the use of the term "Nigger" thrown around; it ran out of their mouths like water from a fountain that does not have a "cut-off" valve.

When you bothered William Washington Sr. or William Washington, Jr., you had to fight the entire Washington family, because they definitely stuck together. Everybody would take a part in the battle from the first to the tenth cousin. Numbers were where the Ku Klux Klan's strength lay. Just by themselves, they did not have the greatest affect. Therefore, strength in numbers was how the black community stood against this adversary.

Even with the strength that the black in the neighborhood had pulling together, there was still a rumbling that was growing below the surface.

CHAPTER 8

A rumbling, like a volcano when it is about to erupt begun to be heard, very low at first, but then it grew to a full-scale eruption. In this sense, the Negro were declined the quest for equality and justice more than once. In addition, the request for justice and equality came back with a big stamp across it that said, "Access Denied." A denial also came from a terrorist group with in the South widely known as the Ku Klux Klan.

Shane stated that, "The rumbling had been far off like thunder that promises that a storm is coming."

Shane said, "The adults in the community were talking with that look of concern on their faces with lots of whispering among the adults and leaders in the community.

Shane said, "This was frightening to small children to see mom and dad and grandpa and others talking and whispering gave her an eerie feeling." Elizabeth and William told their children to stay close to home and not leave the yard. "Why is this, was Shane and her siblings response?"

Shane said "We had always been able to leave the yard, visit the neighbors, go to Grandpa William, Sr. house, and play in the street at night, especially on moonlit nights. Daron, Sharon, Michael, Chester, and Elijah and I talked among ourselves about this sudden loss of freedom. Why was mom and dad being mean and limiting where they could go? Their older sister Daron, seemed to understand a little better than her younger siblings, but even she was at a loss, for a while of what the implications of her parent's actions were."

Ultimately, with sadden faces and broken hearts, naturally the children obeyed, what else were they to do? The other children in the neighborhoods were having the same marching orders: stay close to home and do not go anywhere by yourselves.

As the rumble got closer and louder, even more fear set in. The doors to citizens homes were locked early. The shotgun that was hanging on a rack in Elizabeth and William's bedroom was sat in the corner of the living room by William's chair, curtains to all the windows were closed, which usually was open, the coal oil lamps which were used for lighting those lights were dimmed, so no shadows were cast.

"Everyone spoke quietly so there would be no noise so mom and dad could hear. There were so many changes, too many changes to adjust too in such a short span of time. William would sit up lots of nights, according to Shane; he kinda slept in the recliner with his gun near. Grandpa William and other neighbor men did the same in an effort to protect their families. Daylight seemed to be a long time coming during these nervous times and night was an unwelcome visitor. If night could have had eyes, it would have made Shane and her sibling feel better. At least, with light you can see. Evil lurks in the dark and at night; night had no eyes."

There are two important points to look at when speaking of evil. First: evil turn upon itself and becomes self-destructive in the end. Being destructive by nature, it will destroy anything even itself when there is nothing else to destroy. Second: notice how evil can be used to accomplish God's purpose. According to Revelations 17:17, God's rule and power stands supreme over all the acts of men and angels. Even if we intend things to be evil, God's power and mercy is shown in that it can produce good from the evil: Genesis 50:20; Romans 8:28.

This should comfort all of us. Behind a frowning providence, God hides a smiling face as William Cooper? Said, "God is good, his intentions are good, his will and power is good, and his actions are good. Evil can never stop God's good from being done and in its own peculiar way; evil only cooperated in the accomplishing of God's good will. *http://www.poemhunter.com/poem/god-moves-in-a-mysterious-way/*

The Ku Klux Klan had their parades and meetings. They paraded down the streets and roads with horns blowing, lights blinking and loud calls. Their intended intimidation spread to all the communities both black and white. The law at that time had no legal constraints on the books or written guidelines that made it unlawful for them to hold rallies and parades, in fact, the law enforcement seemed to give them protection and allow parades.

The Washington family had dogs because William was a hunter. He hunted coons, rabbits, turkeys, deer squirrels or any other wild game. The dogs kept up enough noise to warn off any villain. Shane recalled how irritated she would feel with the dogs barking, but at this point, the entire family felt better when they heard the dog bark at night or even the daytime for that matter. It was not as distributing as previously thought, but rather the barking acted as a first line barrier for safety from the ugly monster lurking in the dark, potentially outside any door in the neighborhood.

This monster was a menace to both races, white and black. Especially for black, but, just as much so if someone in the white race was perceived as being a friend of the black race. There were whites in Chunchula and Georgetown that were subjected to the same kind of targeted bias and racism that the blacks were subject to.

Doing what is right has never been too popular with the majority. The majority usually follows the crowd whether they agree or not; there were some of those in the crowd also. The members of the white neighborhood that did not adhere to or agree with the ideology of the Klan were just as afraid of their homes being burned or their families being injured, as the members of the black community was, so they stayed silent publically; but behind the scenes, they were supportive and sympathetic. How can someone live like this not being able to stand on your ethical principles, but rather, let them be decided for you?

In the early days of the ugly monster peaking, its head, Shane said that, "Some of the members of the white community would come by on their so called visit. Now these visits seemed just a little different from the visits that use to take place between the white and blacks in the neighborhood, not that the relations were that good between the two groups.

At this point in the puzzle, there was a cold friendliness and false effort put into their once warmer association. All of the time before the pre-Civil Rights Era, relationships were still tense but not at the level they were once the Civil Rights Movement progressed. Before the Movement started that was always a tolerance with that unspoken societal line always there in place.

There was just almost a thickness in the air, feelings that you could cut with a knife." Shane said, "Her father and mother were careful in what they said to their children so that they would not get the impression that a negative behavior would be acceptable from their children. Shane said her parents said, "There is enough negativity in the world, the Washington family is not going to add to it; they took a wait and see position." Even with the danger for any race, the danger was definitely more eminent for the blacks in the communities. The blacks in the rural area became the "Target" for this monster to gobble-up, if possible.

Even with all the bitterness, the 1960s had a beautiful beginning with "Camelot" on the horizon, the beginning of the Kennedy years, a bright light for the country.

CHAPTER 9

The 1960's was the beginning of the Kennedy years in the White House. These years were promising. President Kennedy had chosen a very appropriate person at his First Lady. First Lady, Jacqueline Bouvier Kennedy gave the Kennedy years the ambiance of a Camelot, King and Queen. It was the creation of a wonderful atmosphere, but all too soon, that hope after a thousand days in office, came to an unexpected and abrupt violent end and the promising Utopia, faded. President Kennedy overcame many daunting task assigned him by virtue that he was the President of the United States, *The Kennedy Years, Viking Press, 1964)*

This era, 1960's began as an era that was full of what America could be; of what was on the horizon for this great country. The new President, with a fresh prospective for a wonderful country the nation had just begun to get its land legs. For many years, America just swam along with the tides or rode out the storms that blew upon these magnificent shores.

Electing John F. Kennedy, Jr. was like a breath, of fresh air being pumped into America. But all too soon, these hopes would be dashed and the wonderful new growth would not be realized, the President was assassinated in November 1963. The 1960's drew to-a-close in civil unrest and racial discontent. This civil unrest remained an underlying factor in this nation. As such, before the 1960s ended, the quest for freedom began as a quiet rumble across the nation, just as the rumble of fear began during the early 1960's. It was especially more prevalent in the outlying areas of Mobile County, an ugly monster began to peak its head. That monster was in the neighborhood with an ideology already imbedded in people's minds, which all too soon this ideology became a reality. Violence is horrible to face; people never knew where the violent acts would come from or from whom it would come.

The 1960s were overshadowed and pledged by a trail, of violence which include the: assassination of: John F. Kennedy, Robert Kennedy, Malcolm X, Medgar Evers, and finally Martin Luther King, Jr. This was a very noticeable loss of five great leaders and freedom fighters of our Century. What horrific times, for America in its growth years.

In this wise, a monster can exist in all forms political, social or emotional. There was one had the heads that formed all three in the political, the social and the emotional spheres and domains in the Chunchula and Georgetown communities.

CHAPTER 10

There was a first detection of the monster's presence. Now, a monster has or can have many heads, but only one body, which is a perfect description of the white supremacy group that invaded Georgetown. Who the head was, no one knew for sure; they could have been anyone in Georgetown or Chunchula. Since the signs and evidences were on the Georgetown side, Shane said, "Everyone in the black neighborhoods, both Chunchula and Georgetown assumed (figured) it was from the Georgetown side, which would prove to be true.

The group, however, seemed to operate in both little country towns; but most of the activity came from the Georgetown side. The Ku Klux Klan, with their boorish attitudes, tried to infringe an mental, social and emotional slavery upon a people like an octopus with long tenacious tentacles, once again, taking them back to a semblance of the same bondage that was fought against, for so long, to be done away with.

The first inkling that the trouble was starting was the testing of the waters. Well, good old Tank got it started. He had the thermometer to gauge the temperature. Tank Jones lived in Georgetown. He was that loud type with his belly showing from under an undershirt that was supposed to be white. He was snagged-toothed; both front teeth were missing. He wasn't called Tank for nothing his size and personality fit him well. He was definitely large and out of shape.

Tank and his brother Jessie made a habit of coming to the black neighborhood with Tank's old Ford truck speeding up and down the highway making loud noises. The first night that he got brave enough to how his loyalty to his group was knocking down all the mailboxes on the highway that were the property of the black citizens of Georgetown. They were all lying down on the ground the next morning this warm fall day in October 1963, first hint of testing the waters.

O'Tank was a loud one. He spokes out about how he felt about the coloreds, as he called it. Tank said in his crude and backwoods way, "Them dar' niggas liv' down the road from us, they'uns shouldn't outa be lowed ta be free ta go anywhere." They need owsun's okay ta walk through this neighborhood; they'd done cross da line."

At that time, the lines were only in the minds of Tank and his entourage. "Niggers need to stay in their place" Shane and her brothers and sisters heard him spout this ugliness as they walked by his house on their way to the corner store on Lott Road.

The owner of the little country store, Mr. Watson, never seemed to care what color the person's skin was; he only saw one color "green" money was his focus.

Shane said, "Her father and mother told them that Mr. Watson would sell anything to anybody. His only bias was if customers did not come in the store. He would then go out of his way to find out 'why they did not come in." On the way back from the corner grocery, there sat Tank with his ugly bulldog he owned called, Midnight. He kept this monster, Midnight, on a chain.

Shane said, "O'Tank taught Midnight to hate blacks. Anytime he saw a black person, he would give Midnight the cue and Midnight would lunge as if he would eat up the world. His red eyes would be blazing and he had teeth that looked like iron bars with a hinge on each side. He could literally tar anything or anyone apart."

Shane and her siblings walked on the other side of the highway as close to the ditch as possible. Shane told me to use my imagination (the fear, the sweat, hearts racing, and the temptation was always there to run) to know how young children felt with this vicious animal only held at bay by a chain and an idiot, who taunted she and her sibling each time they went to the corner store with this danger. Shane said, "Evil lurked everywhere around and was deep seated in Tank and came out in the viciousness of his bulldog, Midnight."

Shane said, "They ran home and told their mother about "O'Tank."" Her response at that time was, "Don't worry about Tank, he just never seemed to have learned any manners." For the most part, O'Tank was known in the black communities as being, a loud-mouthed, vulgar and a very disrespectful young man. Elizabeth said, "His mouth needed washing out with soap."

As the days and months passed during the years of 1962-1963, each night the highway was fuming with noise and calls and name calling, "hey nigga". William, Elizabeth and others, as dark began to fall in the neighborhood, would dim the lamps or turn them out period. My dad said Shane, William, Jr. said, "If there are no lights, there are no shadows. You make yourself a target with lights shining and people moving around." "William told his children that whoever was with Tank, like Tank, were cowards. They hid their faces under the cover of darkness of the night. Tank was the "Fido". He was very unpleasant with a contemptible personality. He was out in the forefront of everyone, but without the others to back him, he was not brave enough or smart enough to do any of this dirt on his own."

Elizabeth eventually started hanging quilts and blankets over the windows to mask the light and eliminate the shadows."

Tank and his family lived in what was known as the "curve" on the way to Lott Road. There wasn't anything that was outstanding about his family; they were just a mom and a dad and two sons, Tank and Jessie, who lived in an old white house with beers cans thrown in the yard. Elizabeth, Shane's mother said, "Beer probably contributed to his loud mouth, big belly, and broken teeth. He did not use his God-given common sense or he wouldn't have acted the way he does."

Elizabeth and William, Jr. both said, "We should feel pity for people like Tank and Jessie. Their lives had to have been pretty empty to want to fill it with hate."

This type of experience was not just limited to Chunchula or Georgetown. Before the Civil Rights Movement became a fully blown movement there were rumblings in Selma on a smaller scale even in private owned businesses, like the Watemann Tin Shop. The Tin Man Experience is one example.

CHAPTER 11

Many blacks had "The Tin Man Experience" or one of like nature during these dark and uncertain years. My husband, Timothy, was from Selma, Alabama. He recounted to me stories of race and hate relations among the black and white community. Even though there were no physical lines drawn in the highway as it was in Chunchula, Alabama, there were lines drawn mentally.

The black citizens knew their places and recognized that, as far as Mr. Charlie was concerned, is what the black citizens called the white citizens in Selma. As far as the white citizens were concerned the "Niggers" knew their place and had better stay in it.

He told me about the events surrounding the Watermann's Tin Shop in Selma where he worked for a few years as a young adult under eighteen years of age. There was the boss's son, James the same age of Timothy. He was working there also. They roofed together, laid shingles, worked side-by-side every day during their teen years.

He called James by his first name with no handle on it, just James, no Mr. Watermann or Mr. James. James called him Tim. As is the passing of time, so did the age of two young men, they grew into adulthood. Tim said, "While they were not buddy-buddy, he and James had a pleasant working relationship with frequent interaction on a daily basis."

The winds of change started, as the fall of the year turns into winter, so did the winds of change that blew across the Watermann's Tin Shop. Tim said, "One early morning in August of 1955, the workday started as usual, he thought. He noticed that James did not come in with the rest of the crew. Eight O'clock came around when the office opened, in walked James and Mr. Sam, his father. Both had on suits and ties."

Mr. Sam, the owner, had the Foreman to call all the workers together, who were mostly black. Mr. Sam and James stepped up on the platform outside of the office where he always stood looking down at his workers. Mr. Sam stepped up front and made this grand announcement: "Y'all know my son James, well starting today you can call him Mr. James. He became a man today. He's twenty years old today."

Tim said, "A lump formed in his throat and a lot of the other men's throats that morning as well." James, too, like the winds of change, changed and started using derogative language and racial slurs when he spoke to the workers with whom he worked side-by-side so many years. Tim said that he asked him one day, not long after that ill-fated morning and the suited presentations James and his father made, "Why the sudden change?" Tim said his response was, "My daddy said I am a man now and deserve the respect of my "nigga" workers just like he do." Tim said, "His own response to James statement was silence. He knew that if he said anything or did anything, he would take it too far." As time went on, the winds that bought the change blew even stronger. Tim said, "He continued to work at the Tin Shop, but would not call James, "Mr. James", just James as always."

Tim said, "More than once he was called into the office and warned about breaking the rules of not calling James by his proper title; but decided that he would have to pay with either his dignity, self-respect or his job."

"Tim said, "He worked there until about a month later."

That ill-fated day came, one Friday at pay time, James handed him a pink slip and said, "We don't need you anymore."

Tim said, "He asked them why?" James' response was, "Because you don't respect me like the rest of the nigga workers; you are supposed to call me Mister."

Tim said, "As he contemplated his reply spikes of anger grew in him; after a moment of gaining his composure he said, "You had my respect when you acted like a human being you lost my re*spect* when you elevated yourself above everyone else. Putting Mister before your named and wearing a suit everyday don't gain you any more respect, the character of the man does. In my eyes you've lost both your character and respect."

Tim said, "Though he did not know whether the Watermann's were members of the Ku Klux Klan, but they sure had that pre-dawning supremacy mentality displayed by the Ku Klux Klan."

It takes a lot of strength and dignity for people with Tim's beliefs and values to make a decision and stick by it even though it meant his job and income for that his family could use.

It takes strength, dignity and self-respect to make a decision and stick by it as it was with the women, of the Washington family, especially Elizabeth.

CHAPTER 12

Elizabeth Washington was a portrait of female strength and prowess.

Elizabeth was a model of a strong woman. She did not have a choice. William Washington left home in the mist of all the Civil Rights Era. During the early 1960s, William had to seek employment in the Sugar Cane fields of Louisiana to support his family. This time-period the early 1960s was dangerous and nerve racking.

Shane said, "She was no more than ten years old at that time." Elizabeth was a woman with few advantages or luxuries and conveniences in her life. Rather, she suffered the manacles of hardship that was like a ball and change around her neck, which she carried each day that the sun rose. She was the picture of what we called the disadvantages of being a minority today because of her gender. Surprisingly so, Elizabeth carried this ball and chain of the "disadvantaged" female well.

Shane said, "Elizabeth, her mother, was left with she and her five young siblings: Daron, Sharon, her two older sisters and Chester, Michael, and Elijah, the three younger brothers."

William would be gone for both fall and winter of 1961 and 1962. He would return in April of 1962 just as the Civil Rights Movement was growing. His concerns about his wife and children were justified during his absence.

It was a dangerous time in Chunchula, especially for a woman with six young children. William Sr., was across the road, Shane's grandfather, he helped look after the family while William Jr. was away working. Elizabeth had a code for her children to live by during these perilous times. No one travel singularly, always in numbers preferably, all six at one time. Elizabeth kept William Jr.'s double barrel shot gun in the hall on the gun rack near the dining room and living room for safety purposes.

Shane said her mother's strength stuck in her mind because of the many frequent encounters she had and that she lived through during the time their father was away working in the cane fields in Louisiana. One incident that stands out in Shane's mind was, "A farmer named Mr. Bushfield, who rented other people's fields in the communities if he could, drove up in their yard one day. Elizabeth, as usual, was working with her flowers. He got out of the truck and walked up to her mother and said, "Good morning "Auntie." Shane said her mother stopped pruning her flowers and said, "You never had an aunt that look like me, my name is Ms. Washington. Why are you here in my yard? There is nothing for you here! I am not renting my field this year, as you had been told before." She stood still holding her pruning shears in her hand, firmly looking at him until he got in his truck and left."

Shane said, "After that incident she knew that her mother had the mental strength that it took to stand against adversity and for what she believed was right. She might have been afraid, but she could not tell by her actions."

Everyone in both black and white neighborhoods knew that some of the men were gone for about six to eight months because of the lack of work for blacks at that time, October through March. That winter of 1961-1962 was a hard and cold one, and food was scarce. William Jr. sent money every two weeks, but it still was not enough. Everyone in the neighborhood pulled together to make it. Shane said, "Her mother said, 'Women can do miraculous things when necessary."

There were noises and callings after dark. The danger that existed in the environment was unnerving to Shane. She stayed frightened most of the time. Even though, Elizabeth tried to ease her fears, it did not do any good. The Ku Klux Klan was a fact and they were deep-rooted in the neighborhoods.

The grumbling and rumbling got louder and louder about the Ku Klux Klan. William came home in April of 1962 because of the danger to his family. He did not want to take a chance with his family's safety. Later that year, William turned to farming and raising cotton. It was a successful year for the Washington family as far as crops were concerned. The danger of the Ku Klux Klan remained the same.

There was a tension when the black male populace returned from their jobs away from Chunchula. The white and black citizens passed each other with only a thin line between them. The looks, the tense jaws, the half-clinched fist; it appeared to Shane every minute that there may be a fight. It was definitely one brewing.

Shane heard the talk of more guns than she had ever seen that the black citizens were hiding near their homes. The peace that this once quiet community enjoyed was gone forever. After the tension seem to reach its peak, the black and white lines were being drawn in actuality on the highway.

The Ku Klux Klan, with their boorish attitudes, tried to enforce slavery, once again upon a people, with their long tenacious fingers that would take them back to the same type of bondage that was fought, for so long to do away with.

Therefore, the Spiral of Silence that the black race was under for so long was finally coming to a productive end.

CHAPTER 13

Living in a Spiral of Silence can describe the state that the blacks or colored race was living in for many, many years. The Spiral of Silence reference goes back to the days of slavery, when the black man was stole from his homeland, and forced to come to a country, he knew nothing about to become the property of another man. With the ensuing slavery, silence was part of the requirements. Do what you were told and keep a civil tongue in your head sums up the position of the white slave owners. The people of the black race were seen as having what was called a "place" and they were expected to stay in it. So began the Spiral of Silence.

Elizabeth Noelle Neumann, German Political Scientist, developed the Spiral of Silence Theory(1974), which states, "The one view dominated the public scene and others disappeared from the public awareness as its adherents became silent" which, is a good example, of what happened to the black man as forced aficionados of a position not of their choosing. Fear, separation, and isolation were some of the results of slavery as with a people subjected to living in a Spiral of Silence. *http://masscommtheory.com/category/theory/spiral-of-silence/*

That Spiral of Silence lasted for more than two hundred forty five years from 1619 when the first slaves arrived in America, in Virginia, the year before the pilgrims landed on Plymouth Rock. From that moment, for the next two hundred forty-five years the Negro race was treated in unspeakable ways.

After the death of President Lincoln in 1865, the Thirteenth Amendment passed abolishing slavery. Looking at it from this perspective, the 13th Amendment abolished slavery on paper, but not in reality. The black man was treated in the same way they were before the 13th Amendment was passed. Therefore, the Spiral of Silence continued.

http://www.history.com/this-day-in-history/president-lincoln-dies

In order for life to be bearable, humans will do whatever is necessary to survive. Therefore, the Negro race created their own culture, which they passed down, from generation to generation. Do not do anything to upset the applecart of safety. There was no respect for the black race, as any human would expect to receive from his fellowman, so you create a generation of people that lived and worked in fear and deprived of the decency due anyone. Survival for the black man became an insulated culture. In order to survive the Negro shielded their culture and way of living.

The black man lived in a maze of timidity. Therefore, the Negro was forced by slavery, to become reticent, without freedom of speech or movement, almost like caged animals.

A maze leads you in different uncertain ways with the end of the maze impossible to find so it was with the black race, it was a maze of slavery with no end in sight. No accentuation of words would calm or change what was taking place.

Even after the 13th Amendment was passed abolishing slavery, physical slavery that is; another kind of slavery took its place, a mental slavery, which involved instilling fear into the minds and hearts of the black race. This can be likened to a car that never changes gears, but runs at the same level at all times.

Those words, of freedom were, written in the United States Constitution, but the actual freedom was not there. It can be also compared or contrasted to, a person being underwater and cannot get to the top, even though you can see the shadow of the top, you cannot reach it.

Fast forwarding to the late 1800, when the Ku Klux Klan had its first rise, which bought more of the same "fear and intimidation"; both were on the horizon for the black race. The Ku Klux Klan had its beginning in Pulaski, Tennessee in 1866. The focus of this white supremacy group was to stop blacks from voting. The agony and anguish that the Ku Klux Klan inflicted on the black race was inhuman.

The black community sticking together was that three-cord string that could not be broken, not when they pulled together was a strong force against the mental, emotional and physical slavery that were being thrown at them by the Ku Klux Klan. It was like living in a vacuum, no way out, closed in on all sides with nowhere to go or run. So what do you do? William said, "You turn and fight." Fight not for your safety, but for your dignity and the future of your sons and daughters and their dignity and sense of freedom."

Further, Shane noted, "I believe that when your dignity is gone, because you let it be taken because of fear, then it becomes a part of that Spiral of Silence. That Spiral of Silence is passed down, for generations, which becomes like a falling rock it tumbles until it gets to a stopping point. When hitting the ground the rock just lays, no action and no changes. The same rock will fall the same way when dropped again, so the spiral continues."

Where is the spiral to stop? There must be a common ground found to achieve this, but how?

CHAPTER 14

Finding Common Ground is hard in any situation and easy in others.

In the question of love and understanding, in these, two finding this common ground is the hardest things to do. In contrast, when it comes to race it is almost impossible. The citizens of America, black, white or red had not found this common ground before the Civil Rights Movement, that love and understanding had not found a common ground to grow in not yet. This process would take a helper and a fertilizer.

The black race's cup finally "runneth" over with the successful efforts of Martin Luther King, Jr., and the Civil Rights Movement. That check, that had been presented, so many times over the past hundreds of years to the Bank of Justice was not returned insufficient funds any longer, but rather, it was beginning to be paid in small installments at first and these installment amounts grew as the months and years passed.

In the meanwhile, the equality and unalienable rights that was being put in an escrow account in the minority races name, could finally be drawn on, one check at a time. Martin Luther King, Jr., had leveled the play field in the Civil Rights Movement. Therefore, Common Ground was established.

The South was the battleground for the War Between the States and the battleground for the Civil Rights Movement; the Ku Klux Klan's war on the black race because of their quest for equality. The battle not only took place in a physical sense, but in a mental and emotional sense as well. There was loss of life and there was blood spilled at all levels. However, Slavery was only one of the reasons for the war fought between the States.

The Civil Right Movement was a movement to acquire those equal right won for the Negro by the North winning the war. Those rights for black were frustrated by another war, one of hate and race relations fostered by the Ku Klux Klan. There was no common ground, finding it would be hard, it was needed but how and where?

The idealism of the Ku Klux Klan had encroached itself upon America's South with a child-like spirit, almost unnoticeable, with long tentacles like an octopus as it squeezes the life out of its victims with the suction cup of racism on every tentacle. The South had "black" fertile ground for their idealism to grown in fertilized by the Ku Klux Klan's hatred for a race of people.

With glazed over eyes, America refused to see the terrible acts of which the Klan were capable. That was for someone else to see. The Klan was doing the South a favor by eliminating the black race one way or the other. Wherefore, the idea of keeping the Negro in slavery or getting rid of them either way, it is a form of slavery.

Resolutely, these acts to bring about the elimination of the black race, was their aim in life. Hate has many faces. There were the faces of pretending. The daytime faces; and the faces of revenge and then there was the nighttime face, where all the hate came out whether it was burnings, hangings, or beatings.

The hate from the Ku Klux Klan flowed like the deep murky water of three-mile creek that extends from the Mobile River across half of the city of Mobile. There are a lot, of organisms living in that water in Three Mile Creek. Mostly, there is a very dangerous undercurrent, compared to the undercurrent of the Ku Klux Klan.

Dare we leave out any red blood that ran on these hallowed grounds or any people that shared in the building of a nation?

That Spiral of Silence would continue even though the black race helped to build this nation with their sweat, blood and sacrifice, without any recognition, this is a great "Ponderence."

That common ground is like figuring out the elements or the layers of a preverbal "Pandora's Box." There is so much to try to uncover when trying to dig your way through the muck and mire to find that common ground. Where do you begin in this process?

An Oak Tree, for example can be styled as a common ground. Consider the oak tree standing so strong, tall and proud. This is the way our country did and does stand. That oak tree has many roots, which runs in many directions, but it has only one main root or taproot, which stabilizes that oak tree. As the root of that oak has a common ground, the trunk so does the people of America. The branches of an oak can be compared to, the many people of all races, nationalities and cultures in America.

The trunk of the tree is the strength of America with all the states and its citizens pulling together to make-up the oneness that created the foundation for our society. Therefore, there must be some common ground. That common ground is justice and equality for everyone as stated by the 13th Amendment in the Constitution of the United States. Those roots from the trunk, of the oak tree included: Blacks, Jews, Caucasian, and Native American. The dynamics of freedom as explained by the13th Amendment provided that there can be no difference in equality for American's citizens, if there is a difference it is not to be in equality. *http://www.loc.gov/rr/program/ bib/ourdocs/13thamendment.html*

Another century the same difficulty existed and presented itself as a strong foe, Freedom was the hindrance then as well. Common ground is hard to find or establish; which, was the obstacle that existed between England and America during the Revolutionary War. Freedom of religion was the fleeting point for the pilgrims. The pilgrims had to go where they could find Religious freedom.

In Africa, the black man fled to maintain their freedom. This flee was in vain, they were taken hostage and forced to come to a land that had been founded on the principles of freedom for all men; but that freedom, as time passed , became more illusory. The Ku Klux Klan made a mockery of the rights promised mankind that came to live on this American soil. Here again, another line was drawn, for the black man.

In order to have that common ground, there comes a wading- process first. So many layers, of the Pandora Box had to be waded-through, before finding this common ground.

CHAPTER 15

The background to the story of Pandora's Box is the Titan Prometheus's passive aggression toward the King of the gods, Zeus. Having gotten away with or having paid the price for one misdeed, Prometheus kept going back for more. Zeus was very creative in the way he meted out punishment. Pandora was one example: Prometheus was mankind's benefactor. The king of the gods were not crazy about mankind and did not want man to have among other things, "fire."

Prometheus on the other hand, wanted good things for man, so stealthily he brought man the gift of fire. Zeus presented man with a "gift" Pandora, the first woman. Pandora came from the forge of Hephaestus, beautiful as a goddess and beguiling. Zeus gave Pandora to Prometheus's brother Epimetheus and a box with orders not to open. Pandora, filled with curiosity, opened it and let out the blight and evil. Man would be blighted with illness for a lifetime. *http://ancienthistory.about.com/od/grecoromanmyth1/a/050410Pandora_and_her_box_or_pithos.htm*

Like Prometheus, the Ku Klux Klan had gotten away with their misdeeds for so long it became the norm in the Southern Society. Their evil and hate mainly of the black race kept reaching new heights and new levels. Their misdeeds like Prometheus', was a ticking time bomb. The illusion of supremacy blinded their minds to the point that they could not see that there were growing opposition to their actions.

The Montgomery bus incident opened up a Pandora's Box. When the lid came off everything that was hidden, for generations of being muffled by time and other nitty-gritties such as: injustice and disrespect for the rights of a people, and the overwhelming cruelty of one segment or faction of a race for another, these facts and elements were alarming.

The contents of that Pandora's Box was old and musty and deteriorated by time. Nothing had changed no way out, so nothing fresh could come in, everything remained status quo. It had finally come apart and all the contents. Yes, these contents were pulled out one at a time. Contents like:

racism, cruelty, anger, violence, and hatred. Love and caring were not two of the emotions that were found in this box. What variety of items were in a Pandora's box that had been shut-up for a long time could not be determined without opening it; therefore, no one knew what to expect. The 1960's Civil Rights March and Movement turned into a major deal. The muck and mire necessary to be waded through in this box would take a Civil Rights Movement. Shane said, "A movement in this wise, is defined as going from one point to another."

The movement started with the simple act of refusal to give up a seat, but even before then, there were private movements. Shane said, "What came to her mind was the Underground Railroad movement in the 1780-1862 year with people being led to the North in a quest for simple freedom. http://www.pbs.org

In the 1960's Martin Luther King, Jr., led another freedom March to the North from the South. The trial of tears is a glaring reality for the black race. This was another of the "bad" that was pulled from that Pandora's Box of blight.

The affliction of being in turmoil and distress every day of your life is almost unimaginable. Shane noted that, "There are causes of turmoil and stress that are unavoidable it is called living; but, when this is the case, that these afflictions are enforced upon a race of people, because of the color of your skin, it is more than unbearable. This left a stain on the whole of the nation's system of justice and equality.

A stain that should always stand as a reminder of where this nation was and where this nation is now in reference to pulling the bad out of the Pandora Box's. Have we gotten down to all of the good yet? Or, do we still have a ways to go? This stain should cause us to question ourselves and score ourselves and see what our scorecard says."

Likewise, being granted equal rights and freedom to move about as free citizens, not have the feelings, of being threatened or maligned because of the color of their skins or their cultural beliefs and values are important freedoms to have. The Civil Rights Movement pulled four hundred and sixty-five years of bad from the Pandora's Box of injustice. http://afroamhistory. about.com/od/timelines

The Pandora's Box held such biases as the Spiral of Silence, the back-doorism, the back-seatism, the name-calling, the stereotyping, and more that the black race had suffered and been exposed too, for so long. To pull from the Pandora Box all of the blight of injustice that was been packed into it, for four hundred sixty- five years could go on for an eternity. Looking at access to true freedom in this way would seem like an eternity. Therefore, the justice system of America performed a "blanket" removal of the bad; they scraped down through the bad until the good started to shine through.

It only took one person making that first step across a line that had been drawn centuries ago and found in the blights of the Pandora's Box. Rosa Parks was that one person that cried out for justice by her act of crossing that line.

CHAPTER 16

Rosa Parks took that step and cross that color line. Thus, bringing its long-reaching arm of torture to the early and late 1950's and Montgomery, Alabama and North Mobile County. A significant day in the history of America, especially the South when Rosa Parks set off a ripple that reached across America and into every household. Her refusal to give up her seat to a white man started the ripple. The door was finally opened that had not been opened before, of this magnitude anyway. "If opportunity doesn't knock, build a door, *Milton Berle*."

This quote mirrored that one act by Rosa Parks. The door was built when The United States Constitution and the Emancipation Proclamation was penned, which these two documents were the fore runners for this opportunity to make a change for equality.

Rosa Parks step across a color line and unlatched that door and the Negro stepped through it. http://www.ushistory.org/us/54b.asp

Ms. Parks was not a celebrity figure at that time, just a citizen riding home after a long day's work ended. Why could a citizen not be able to sit down after a hard day's work, if you are tired? But, no this was not a privilege granted the black race, not even hardly at the back of the bus, if a white passenger wanted to sit. Then you stand up and hold on to a pole. This was not only happening in Montgomery, but in every southern city in America.

There was a holding on to a remnant of the ideology of slavery, "let the white man go first." But, Mrs. Parks single act broke that Spiral of Silence that had enslaved the black race for more than three hundred years; this act set the black race on a different road to true freedom and not a black and white freedom, one that was written on paper in years long past. Not necessarily, the freedom to walk around, but the simple freedom of humanity; to be treated with respect and dignity as any free citizen of this great nation would expect to be treated, rather than treat a race of people as if they were still slaves both mentally and physically.

The key to unlocking the chains of injustice, equality, fairness and freedom, was among a race of people who had the heart to stand and demand payment for an insufficient fund check that was presented more than once to the Bank of Justice of America.

The chains that bound this race of people left scars that extended for decades beginning in 1675 and lasted until the late 1950's and early 1960's when Rosa Parks stood for her rights to sit. This single act started a domino effect of events that resounded, was like the "Shot" heard around the world.

This great act turned the tides and unlocked the chains that bound the Negro and started them on the true road to freedom in real time and not on paper. This paper freedom that patronized the Negro, patted them on the head like you would a child that asked for a snack to close to dinner. When you tell them no, pat them on the head and say run along until after dinner and ask me again later. No pacificity or too much pacificity is akin to giving the Negro forty acres and a mule.

These ideas reinvented a territorial fight for whose land it is, that was one of the points. These points of ownership was decided during the Civil War; all that was necessary after that was to move forward with freedom, for everyone on an equal basis. There was no real time mentality about freedom here, just injustice. Freedom is a language even babies understand. Warmed over justice prevents forward movement, it only comes after the debris of injustice is bulldozed out of the highway, only then can successful freedom is achieved.

This was not the case not while children suffered this injustice and paid for this injustice with the loss of their life or paid as, they suffered through the fear and seed of uncertainty that were planted in them, by the events and circumstances that were taking place in all around them. The loss of the Birmingham 4 is a case in point. What would these children of this contemptible act say if they could? Shane said, "She could imagine that children all over the South, was feeling the pain of this heinous act of bombing the Sixteenth Street Baptist Church in Birmingham, Alabama on a Sunday morning, which did not help the level of fear already present in their minds."

CHAPTER 17

The Birmingham and 16th Street Baptist Church sticks out like a sore thumb in this Civil Rights movement.

According to Tyson (1963) Birmingham was a haven to the South's most violent Ku Klux Klan chapter. Birmingham was probably the most segregated city in the country. Dozens of unsolved bombings and police killings had terrorized the black community since World War II. The 16th Street Baptist Church was a known place for the meeting of civil rights leaders such as Martin Luther King, Jr, Ralph Abernathy and Fred Shuttleworth. Tension became high when the Southern Christian Leadership Conference (SCLC) and Congress of Racial Equality (CORE) became involved.

According to Tyson (1963) on September 15, 1963 a white man was seen getting out of a white and turquoise Chevrolet car and placing a box under the steps of the Sixteenth Street Baptist Church. Soon afterwards, at 10:22 a.m., the bomb exploded and killed Denise McNair (11), Addie Mae Collins (14), Carole Robertson (14), and Cynthia Wesley (14). The four girls had been attending Sunday school classes at the church. Twenty-three, other people were also hurt by the blast.

http//www.english.illinois.edu/maps/poets/m_r/randall/Birmingham.htm

Killing innocence is heinous. These young people went in innocent and unaware that any such danger existed at their church. Shane said, "Their parents sent them off to Sunday school, as any parent would on a Sunday morning, with the knowledge that they were at least safe at church. They considered this at least a safe place, a sanctum, a refuge of safety, to at least, serve God in peace."

The Cahaba Group known as the Ku Klux Klan's splinter group was the one's that carried out the bombing; this fact was not revealed until the year 2000 by the FBI (Tyson, 1963).

Thirty-seven years is a long time to wait to have a crime solved that took the lives of a total of 4 innocence children and injured twenty- three others that dark day in Birmingham, Alabama. Shane said, "This story reminded her of the group that was operating in the rural areas in Mobile County. The fear that goes with this type of malice is almost unreal. When this story was heard on her parent's radio added not only to the sadness that already existed in her family for the injustices that was happening across the South in both inner city and rural areas." Shane said, "She and her sibling just felt like hiding all the time. At that time, her thoughts were how she, her family and other families would make it through these terrible times? Will their parents be okay? Each morning that her father left the house to go to work those knots in her stomach got tighter, she prayed, God, please don't let my daddy get hurt, let him come home again."

So much pain existed in families that lived in the black communities everywhere across the South. However, when you involve children in your hate it takes on a different color connotation and a different meaning.

Shane said, "The parents of the Birmingham 4's pain ran much deeper than she could even imagine." Just knowing how her parents felt about their children and their safety she could somewhat identify with the feelings they had." It hurts when your target is anyone, but the whole of the matter for the Ku Klux Klan was the black race and their not voting and having equal rights provided by the Constitution of the United States. The Ku Klux Klan was like a dangerous inferno consuming everything in their path. In Birmingham as well as in Chunchula and in Georgetown, their path only led to the door of the Negroes and their helpers.

Shane told me that, "She always believed until this day that the bomb was meant for the Civil Rights leaders that met at the Sixteenth Street Baptist Church and not for those children." Acts of violence always involve more than just the person that you are targeting. There are always innocence bystanders or ones that are unaware of the looming danger.

The children of Birmingham, Mobile, Montgomery, Selma, and every nook and cranny where there were Negro children felt the knots and pain in their stomachs. Shane said, "It is an insurmountable fear that consumes your whole being and creates an environment of fear of every noise and everyone you meet. Children cannot put into place a rational, for the acts of violence against other children or their parents. They seldom understand why someone would want to hurt them or their parents.

As a child, you cannot reason with the knots in your stomach and that sick feeling so intense that your whole body reacts to it." Shane said, "It caused nose bleeds to vomiting in her, she as just sick with fear and dread." Shane said, "She had to sleep between her mother and father because of these nose bleeds and the fear that tied her stomach in knots. There was an enormous pressure weighing down on her mind about the danger that was ever-present. Her parents became a shadow of safety for Shane.

The city of Birmingham is traumatized forever because of four innocence girls and a heinous act of violence perpetrated by a political racist group with a propensity for violence to accomplish a mission that could not feasibly, come-to-pass. Elimination of a race of people by man, is a fallacy, it has been since the beginning of time.

Birmingham, today is a different city it has come into its own, electing political leaders of all races, creeds and colors and the citizens seem to live a more peaceful life than was had less than forty years earlier during the Civil Rights Movement, but look at the price paid for their peace. This peace costs the lives of four innocent children who we can label as victims, as well as, how many others that are unwritten and unknown, those unsung heroes on a battleground in a fight for freedom and the sacrifices they and their families did not make. Michael Donald was an example of this type of sacrifice: a mere child not even out of his teens.

Shane said, "An example of what she thought of was the children in Mississippi during the disappearance of the three young Civil Rights workers. Burning, hanging, hatred, and bitterness cannot even begin to describe what took place during the time between the arrival and disappearance of these young people. How did this affect the children in Mississippi, especially when you are part of this hatred?"

CHAPTER 18

The account of the disappearance of the Civil Rights workers are portrayed well in the movie the Mississippi Burning. *http://www.imdb.com/title/tt0095647/*

As time went on, and the laws of America saw no reason to restrain the action of the Ku Klux Klan, they became out of control. The movie, "The Mississippi Burning", is a good true-to-life depiction of what the environment was like with this monster present. Gene Hackman, did an excellent job of portraying the FBI agent who successfully extracted the truth about the identity of the local leader of the Ku Klux Klan and who was doing the killings in the black community. There is always "one" that will turn over on a group of this sort or a whistle blower in the organization either someone with inside information or someone that had infiltrated the group.

So dangerous was this type of chance that the infiltrator or whistle blower would not be identified; they would live in horrible fear of the inevitable. The chance was great of being discovered and if discovered it meant a horrible unspeakable death for that individual. If this type of danger existed in the inner cities of the South, it existed even more in the rural area of the surrounding towns. The citizens of these towns were afraid, so the Spiral of Silence continued; but, even with a spiral, there is an end.

A spiral is a downward motion, an action or mentality passed on from generation to generation. Humans often live in a spiral of silence, much like a bird caught in a net, the more it struggle the more entangled it becomes. Man does the same or acts in the same manner, acceptance is the ultimate end of the bird tanged in a web of silence and acceptance will be the ultimate end of a race of people caught in a spiral of silence, also a type of slavery.

Therefore, a race of people that think that they have no choice, but to suffer in silence is a people who have no hope. Likewise, suffering in silence is an inward emotion. This type of suffering cannot be seen outwardly nor is it displayed outwardly by that man. Therefore, this suffering continues and eats away at the very soul of the inward man or the race of people destroying any foundation that might have supported them as a race of people or even an individual, for that matter. The spiral of silence continued until Rosa Parks spoke up for her rights to sit after a long day's work to just simply ride home on public transportation that her taxes help pay for.

Many fallen heroes before Mrs. Parks had tried to break that silence, for example Megger Evans, who paid a dear price for that attempt, with his life. *http://www.naacp.org/pages/naacp-history-medgar-evers*

A Spiral of Silence defines a dismal condition or state to exist in, most certainly, one that would be despised any human. Shane said, "This reminded her of a quote she heard and later read. Her parents spoke of this as she grew and learned about life outside of her father and mother's home. It was a quote by the Poet Langston Hughes." The quote is as follow: "Negroes sweet and docile, meek, humble, and kind: beware the day they change their mind." The black race started to fight back; sweet, docile, meek, humble, and kind was disappearing.

Those mind-sets that had become natural to the Negro were changing, evident as Hughes said, "They had changed their minds, enough is enough, where will it end?" It only ends, if an end is put to it. Hence, like a pattern that need the excess trimmed before it can be used to make a garment; so, the pattern for these new rights to change and speak up for self, the excess had to be trimmed from around it before it could be used to make new garments of self-expression.

Every human has the desire to be free, live free, walk free, and be free to think for themselves and make their own decisions based on human rights to freedom. If we live under the Constitution of the United States, we have the same rights. Spiral of Silence, no matter the condition or environment, it is based on, is a degrading human condition based either on fear or human suppression of another human or the inability to speak out because they are not sure of themselves as effective communicators.

The Ku Klux Klan, without right, placed the Negro/black race under a twisted type of censorship that emanated from their actions toward people of different color, belief, values, ideology, and from what the Ku Klux Klan believed people should be. According to Langston Hughes, "Race begins at the color line." www.PoemHunters.com

If the Negro had not been available for the outpouring of hate and dissension, which the Ku Klux Klan exhibited toward them, there would have been some other race just as Haman targeted the Jews in Biblical times. Just the thought that anyone would have the gall to insinuate themselves upon another is contemptible.

Minna Antrim (author) said, "*To know one's self is wisdom, but to know one's neighbor is genius.*" There was one that knew herself and what she wanted her life to be like. She started a domino effect with that one "refusal" which broke that spiral of silence.

Up to the point that Rosa Parks stood up and broke that spiral of silence, nothing was done about the bias and prejudice directed at the black race.

According to Johnson (2006), "Prejudice can be defined as an unjustified negative attitude toward a person based solely on that individual's membership in a particular group. Prejudices are judgments made about others that establish a superiority/inferiority belief system. If one person dislikes another simple because that other person is a member of an ethnic group, sex, or religion, that is prejudice. One common form of prejudice is ethnocentrism, which is the tendency to regard our own ethnic group, culture, or nation as better or more correct than others", p.546.

Oh, there were sympathizers, just as there were before the Civil War. The sympathies for the condition of the black race were in silence, as well as, behind closed doors. This type of sympathy is self-serving, an explanation or justification to a guilty conscience. So the spiral of silence continues even in the white race, therefore it was not confined to one people or race.

With the Negro being in-prisoned in this spiral of silence, because of fear, it becomes after a while, a dream deferred. This dream of freedom that had been right out of reach was getting dimmer and dimmer. What is the difference in the bonds of slavery that had been their lives for hundreds of years? Whether physical or emotional – results are the same. The Negro had to wait for that dream. Langston Hughes said, "*What happens to a dream deferred, does it dry up like a raisin in the sun? Or does it explode? A dream deferred is a dream not lived.*" That dream was drying up as a raisin in the sun. The black man lived in a white run world and, until Rosa Parks crossed that line, that dream would stay dried up. But, the raisin did not just dry up, it exploded into that desire to have those inalienable rights that the Preamble to the Constitution spoke of that was penned by the Forefathers of the nation for everyone. It was an edict and stated as:

"We the people of the United States in order to form a more perfect union establish justice, insure domestic tranquility, provide for the common defense, promote the general welfare, and secure the blessing of liberty to ourselves and our posterity, do ordain and establish the Constitution of the United States of America."

Preamble to The United States Constitution, 1789

http://www.senate.gov/civics/constitution_item/constitution.htm

A perfect union is everyone and not limited to some. A select few or the few that an organization decides is not worthy to be part of that great union. Martin Luther King, Jr., spoke of the Constitution and its relation to what was happening in the 1960's during the Civil Rights Movement. "The Negro had been issued a check by the bank of justice that check was bad and came back marked insufficient funds." One could hardly believe that in a nation as large and as rich as America is, that there was not enough riches of justice to go around to all races. The Negro made up part of that perfect union.

They help build the nation with lots of sacrifices: sweat, blood, loss of love ones to death and the auction blocks of the South. When we owe a debt, we are obligated to pay. A check presented to a bank stamped insufficient funds, because the bank cannot honor it is scary. The bank of justice that could not pay was hurting the entire nation…this injustice became a "monkey" on America's back weighing down the system of justice.

Michael Donald was one evident of a justice system that began to pay a debt long over-due to a race of people. The "monkey" on the back of equality and justice, for all was finally tested. Fair and equal justice, was finally served to the group behind this heinous crime, for the unnecessary loss of an innocent young life. In 1970, justice and equality finally reached the corner so it could turn.

CHAPTER 19

Looking forward to the early 1970's, Michael Donald, was the corner turned for the justice system that had failed the Negro race more than once. A simple human right such as walking was not even free. Blacks were not free to walk where they wanted to Michael Donald was a case in point for this simple function. All men have the right to walk down the street; it is a God-given right.

Was Michael Donald was in the right place at the right time? *Definitely, there is no wrong place at the wrong time when you are at home.* The Ku Klux Klan took it upon themselves with what they called keeping black people in their place and what they called justice, was an eye for an eye; just another scare tactic, their forte'. How do you go from being a political force to stop a people from voting to being a terrorists group to rid the world of what they call that race of undesirable people?

This could have been any family in the South. Every family no matter who they were could identify with the pain and heartache caused with this senseless plunder. No death of a human being by another human being should equal one of this magnitude because, of the racial issues and dislike for another race.

The Ku Klux Klan was a cancer until, their actions were checked by the authorities; a heinous crime of proportion had to be committed that caught the nation's attention. It bought the issue of race and bias of the Ku Klux Klan to the forefront, but not until the murder and finally the hanging of an innocent nineteen years old, teenager.

Michael Donald Avenue sits off Spring Hill Avenue, in the heart of town. When driving down Spring Hill Avenue look to the right, there sits a constant reminder. The street sign is labeled: "Michael Donald Avenue"; it is hard not to think of the vigilante band of terrorists and what they did; and the innocence of this young man cut down in the prime of his life depriving his mother of the joy of having a son, for more than just nineteen years. There were a lot, of nineteen year olds sons among the Negro citizens in Mobile County. Shane recalled her mother saying that, "Her fear was that three of her sons were at Citronelle High School, newly integrated, this could have happened to any woman's son, any mother would fear for their son or their daughters, for that matter."

Photo of Michael Donald Avenue

Michael Donald Avenue stands symbolically as a reminder of this terrible tragedy and depredation of an innocent young man's life. His family was left with the pains of suffering this devastating lost, that left a void in their family and ultimately their heart.

As with any evilness, criminal charges were press against the perpetrator (s); justice was administered. Thankfully, all the fires of retribution are not in the hereafter, but some come immediately and some down the road, in the distant future, no matter who does the harm or injustice. The Michael Donald case proved this so. It was the beginning-of-the end for the Ku Klux Klan's power structure, not in Mobile only, but across the nation.

The miasma of fear was dissipating, as a vapor on a sunny summer morning. And, the Ku Klux Klan's retribution was finally here; not a retribution based on violence, but in a peaceful manner; a persistent type of retribution with the end-results as peaceful as the beginning.

Martin Luther King, Jr., was not a purporter of violence, but rather a purporter of peace. The Negro's winter of discontent was passing into history. Like the Cherokee Nation, their trail of tears had its end. Finally, the home the Cherokee Nation longed for was in sight. For the black race the home of justice, equality, freedom and peace were finally possible after so long a journey. Every road has to end somewhere and sometime. We are not at the end yet, but nearing…And, so, the quest continues.

No matter the resistance from small camps that pops up along the way on the "Road to freedom," everyone must press forward, unwavering in the quest for true freedom. This quest will continue throughout the life of man. The quest did not just begin with the black race, but long ago in ages past, far beyond these magnificent shores. That foundation for the "quest" for freedom was laid by other races held in bondage or slavery, whether that slavery was man-made or self-made.

According to Buckley (2012) Michael Donald's body was hung on a Camphor tree on what was known at that time as Herndon Avenue off Springhill Avenue in Mobile, Alabama (the street has been since renamed Michael Donald Avenue in his honor). *Buckley, L. Michael Donald Lynching 30 Years Later. Lagniappe. http://classic.langiappemobile.com/articel.asp?, October 18, 2012*

The hanging of this nineteen years youth was a heartbreaking moment for the entire city and county. The pictures of this youth hanging from a tree was taken by onlookers and there across the street stood the culprit in this hanging, a member of the Ku Klux Klan, Henry Hayes, who kept a one-bedroom apartment across the street from where the body was found. His father, Benny Hayes was a high-ranking member of the Ku Klux Klan; in fact, he was second in command. How do you cover your tracks from such an incident as this? *http://www.aaregistry.org/historic_events/view/ku-klux-klan-brief-biography*

Any path the Ku Klux Klan traversed, spelled heartbreak and trouble for someone. No mother should have to suffer through this kind of pain and heartache. Someone so young with all his life before him, hung at the hands of an organization that had wreaked havoc across the South.

Shane said, "To try to think or imagine how this child might have felt when he was taken, tortured and then killed, is beyond imagination. She imagined more than knots formed in his stomach and his heart raced out-of-control. Shane said, "She tried to put herself into a situation of this sort; she found it impossible to do, it scared her to death just thinking about it."

After this heinous act, the Ku Klux Klan suffered a vacuum in their organization. There were no hands reaching anymore to pull the Ku Klux Klan out of the hole that they had fallen into with their attacks on the black race in the South, at an escalated rate, which kept growing, seemingly, every day. More octopus-like tentacles seem to grow form that cold head all the times with eyes and no heart and nor feelings were ever shown. They became a destructive machine gobbling-up equality, justice and peace from the Negro race and any other supporters out there.

After the death of Michael Donald that vacuum widen and the hole got deeper and all the hands disappeared that once offered support. When there is no fertilizer to feed the roots of a tree, the limbs and leaves die, so it was with the Ku Klux Klan's influence.

That single act, hanging Michael Donald, was the beginning-of-the-end of the strong influence and the strangle hold of fear and despair that the Ku Klux Klan had laid over the South like a blanket lays on a bed; a blanket covers the entire bed and hang over the sides. Unless, someone remove the blanket; it stays in the same position without change.

According to Honi (2009) the wrongful death of Michael Donald was the beginning of the end of the Ku Klux Klan. *http://www.preservationnation.org/ magazine/2009/todays-news/mobile-african-american-trail.html*, February 24, 2013

Departmentalization is for organizations and universities for the convenience of running a business so employees will know their function or for teaching subjects so students can learn by subject. This is not for people or human beings. How do you departmentalize a races of people, which do you eliminate to increase efficiency? Sounds like a business, planning to downsize?

Subsequently, human beings cannot, be treated like departments in a business. This type of thinking is cold and calculating, which fits the personality and characteristics of the Ku Klux Klan. Eliminating a department in a business or separating departments in academia is feasible. As such, this is not feasible or practical for human beings when you eliminate one race you eliminate the other.

We are all tied together by one blood Adam's the father of all mankind, which includes all of mankind no matter the race, creed, color, or natural origin. The human race had its beginning in the Garden of Eden. Genesis 1:26: "And God said, let us make man in our image, after our likeness"; Genesis 2:18: "And the Lord God said, "It is not good that the man should be alone; I will make him an help meet for him." *Master Study Bible, King James Version, 2001*

The Supreme Court struck down the use of this language of race and bias; however, but Alabama did not for forty years, eliminate the language. This language grew as a canker sore in the Constitution until the year 2000 and election when citizens finally voted it out only by a narrow margin of 2% (51-49%). Two percent is a small margin to eliminate the racist language to give rights to all people; but nonetheless victory is victory no matter the size. *http:// www.constitutionalreform.org/*

The language used in this bid for reform is convoluted and disguised, which does not give the public a clear view of the relation the wording has to race and equality. The Alabama Constitution is a post-reconstruction racism and classicism giving strength to a ruling minority. *http://www.constitutionalreform.org/*

This was the drawing of another color line for the ruling minority. There has never seemed to be the majority of the citizens, just those in power that had the power to say yea or nay. Imagine a Constitution so designed too almost punish rather than, a Constitution that would lead to positive change for all citizens in Alabama.

As with any season, there is an end, so it was with the miasma of fear spread by the Klan for so long it is almost unimaginable to try to count the days. The Negro, as with the Azalea Bushes, of the South both has roots that are embedded deeply and both will bloom in their seasons.

The roots of oak trees, as with the roots of the Negro race, are strong and sturdy. The Negro race had finally started to bloom, as does the Azalea Bushes. Their many winters of fear and discontent had passed and the time for budding was here; fertilized by the Civil Right Movement their full blossoming was a realization.

Looking at the shackles from the past can paint a picture for all to see allowing us to stand and look at what the past was like in the questions of race, justice and equality. Sometimes revisiting our past can help avoid getting off the main track to true freedom and justice for all.

CHAPTER 20

Shackles of the past revisited is a layer of Pandora's Box. America once shackled with oppression from the British, threw it off – only to let those chains fall upon another race of people. America had a universal credo; not only in this country, but in other countries as well, it was the Declaration of Independence, "All Men are created equal" was not a misprint, but man did not apply the inference correctly, apparently. *http://www.archives.gov/exhibits/charters/declaration.html*

Attempting to destroy races of people did not just begin. History records, that Hitler tried to "erase" the Jewish nation. Hitler said, in a letter on September 16, 1919 to Adolf Gemlich, "To begin with, Jewry is unqualifiedly a racial association and not a religious association.... Its influence will bring about the racial tuberculosis of the people." *http://www.jewishvirtuallibrary.org/jsource/ Holocaust/hitler_on_Jews.htmlHitler*

The Bible tells in that Haman tried to annihilate all Jews: men, women and children, Esther 3: 5: When Haman saw that Mordecai would not kneel down to pay him honor, he was enraged. Yet having learned who Mordecai's people were, he scorned the idea of killing only Mordecai. Instead, Haman looked for a way to destroy all Mordecai's people, the Jews, throughout the whole kingdom of Xerxes. Pharaoh with his decree to destroy all the Hebrew male children, Exodus 1: 11, 15, & 22: So the Egyptians came to dread the Israelites and worked them ruthlessly. They made their lives bitter with hard labor in brick and mortar and with all kinds of work in the field; in all their hard labor the Egyptians used them ruthlessly. When you help the Hebrew women in childbirth and observe them on the delivery stool, if it is a boy, kill him; but if it is a girl, let her live. Then Pharaoh gave this order to all his people: "Every boy that is born you must throw into the Nile, but let every girl live." *Master Bible, King James Version, 2001*

So it was, with the Ku Klux Klan in the South tried to destroy the black race.

Christian, (2002) in his article on African-Centered Perspective on White Supremacy quoted Browder (1993) Throughout the last four and a half centuries, racism and white supremacy have continually threatened the existence of African people before, during, and after enslavement. These threats have forced African to modify their beliefs, thoughts, and behavior in order to survive on a planet where they are regarded as "Third World" people. Those who now claim to be members of "First World" are actually late comers to the human family, p. 3. *Journal of Black Studies, November 2002*

There are many Haman's in the world, or symbols of what the Haman's of the world were like. The Ku Klux Klan was the 20th century 'Haman's, Hitler's and Pharaohs all rolled into one. Annihilation of the black race was a throwback to times gone by when other races and nations were on the brink of annihilation, the Ku Klux Klan's focus was the black race, men, women and children, as was seen by the hanging of the murder and hanging of the young victim Michael Donald, targeted because he was black and convenient.

He was murdered in another county to perform the eye-for-an-eye, because, a white person was killed by a black person. Michael Donald was not in the neighborhood where this murder was committed. *http://classic.langiappemobile. com/articel.asp? October 18, 2012*

Just as Haman was, the dust bowl that swept over the Jews in antiquity, so the Ku Klux Klan was the dust bowl of the South that swept over the different races choking the life out of them, there was no part of these people's lives, that their equal rights became "equal rights."

However, Freedom is not a hand-me-down. Hand-me-downs are good among siblings in a family, in reference to clothes, but when it came to freedom from any kind of slavery no matter what it is or why, this hand-me-down freedom is so-called equality and justice, like old clothes with holes in them, this hand-me-down freedom was moth eaten and useless. The purpose it served was giving the black race or any other race subject to slavery by the hands of man more of the same, which is not freedom, equality or justice.

Shane said, It seemed to her that The Ku Klux Klan mimicked what Supreme Leader Ali Khamenei called Israel a "cancerous tumor that should be cut and will be cut." *http://online.wsj.com/home-page*, October 15, 2012

The Klan seemed to have a plan of elimination for any race other than theirs. The black race under "siege" is an analogy of what was taking place. The Klan's attacks seemed to rise and fall, but during those down times, they maintained a dual heritage of hate and violence. The roll call of races or cultures to be eliminated included, but were not limited to African Americans, White Americans (who stood for the blacks) Catholics, Jews, Native Americans and different groups of immigrants. This was due to the rapid social and cultural changes of the world we live in.

Genocide of blacks was the aim of the Ku Klux Klan as they became active during the 1960's Civil Rights Era (in 1866 there were 40 different factions of the Ku Klux Klan). Propaganda was one of the two edged swords used to instill fear in the neighborhoods. http://archive.adl.org/learn/ext_us/kkk/default.asp , October 16, 2012

Shane said her mother and father said, "No one knew who the members of the Klan were; they were well-hidden under the disguise of being prominent members of the community with their fashionable suits, fine cars and homes. They sat each Sunday in church as any good church-going religious people would. The Ku Klux Klan's race and hate heritage, just like ancestry, is passed down, to the next generation, to continue being carried-out. The main-focus of the Ku Klux Klan's organization was, hate and violence. The blacks in the South and (those that supported them) lived in the shadow of intolerance in the eyes of the Ku Klux Klan."

Shane said, "She questioned her parents as to why they used the cross as their symbol to represent their organization." She said, "They told her that the Klan thought they were doing Jesus a favor."

They dare to compare or contrast themselves to the Savior of the World. Christ does not need help with anything that man can envision. They do not know how to punish or correct. Who decides what races of people lives on this earth? Certainly not the Ku Klux Klan. Life and its continuation are in the hands of God. According to Job the 12th Chapter, "Who knoweth not in all this that the hand of the Lord hath wrought this? In whose hand is the soul of every living thing, and the breath of all mankind." Job 12:9-10. *Master Study Bible, King James Version, 2001.*

Puffed-up in their minds, they went about spreading their poison and propaganda throughout the South, where their man operation was head-quartered or where their stumping ground was located. With approximately 5,000 to 8,000 member strong, any organization of this size can spread a lot of hate and commit many acts of violence. *http://www.splcenter.org/get-informed/ intelligence-files/ideology/ku-klux-klan*

These were extreme measures taken by humans against their fellowman. Extremist in Shane's mind from an adult perspective, is a group of people or an organization that go either too far to the left or too far to the right with their ideals or actions. Too far either way can be bad, another layer of Pandora's Box. Life requires that there must be a balance, too far either way, can be deadly and irreversible; from this perspective, like everything else in life, there is an end.

Pandora's Box had a beginning and an end. After wading through all the bad, the final item in Pandora's Box was a gift, a wonderful gift.

Shane said, "After the 1960's Civil Rights Era started and the actions of the Ku Klux Klan was revealed, it was finally despised by the majority of Americans. This revelation bought the desire for peace, and harmony begin; which was the beginning of the end of the Klan grip of hate and violence on the South. The desire had to be there first. All the years before, the desire for a "united" America that respected the freedom and justice for all people, was not there. A desire for status quo seemed to be more prevalent than the desire for change and equality for all people. The desire for change had to come with a new perspective of who the "We" are in the Preamble to the Constitution."

"We the people of the United States in order to form a more perfect union." *Preamble to the Constitution of the United States, 1786 http://www. usconstitution.net/const.html*

The "We" was black, white, and Indians, at that time not just one race. The end of Pandora's Box of injustice, lack of freedom, and lack of equality put America on a new course to true justice, freedom and equality for everyone, regardless of race, creed or culture.

Shane said she thought after she got a full understanding that, "The Ku Klux Klan's association with what Christianity was about and their proposed relationship with Christ our Lord and Savior, was at best, warped and delusional; their belief about the relationship was contradictory to what our Savior said in the scripture."

Christ does not deal with man at that level, but as the Bible states, "There is no respecter, of person with God. Then Peter opened his mouth, and said, "Of a truth I perceive that God is no respecter of person, but accepts men from every nation who fear him and do what is right, Acts:10:34. "There is no Greek, Jew, Syrian, bond or free, but all are alike in Christ." There is neither Jew nor Greek, there is neither bond nor free, there is neither male nor female: for ye are all one in Christ Jesus. And if ye be Christ's, then are ye Abraham's seed, and heirs according to the promise." Galatians 3:28-29. *Master Study Bible, King James Version, 2001*

Paul reminds us that, "We are made from one blood; Acts 17:26: And hath made of one blood all nations of men for to dwell on all the face of the earth, and hath determined the times before appointed, and the bounds of their habitation (Noah and Adam) and have pre-appointed bounds and times." *The Master Bible, King James Version, 2001*

Everyone has the right to move around freely while they live, making choices as they choose.

In this light The Ku Klux Klan had what could be considered to be a racist posture. The Ku Klux Klan took on a Communistic overtone, which they tried to lace their ideologies with religion, using the same philosophical rhetoric that Hitler used when he annihilated the Jewish people. There was no logic in Hitler or the Ku Klux Klan's actions against one specific race of people.

http://www.bbc.co.uk/history/people/adolf_hitler February 22, 2013

There were always incidences and irritations that kept emotions and feeling running at a peek at all time during those years, was Shane's comment to me. Riding the Greyhound bus to Mobile was one of those irritant and very uncomfortable. This ride was commonly referred to as the "Hound."

CHAPTER 21

Riding the Hound to Mobile on Saturdays for shopping at its best was a trying experience. Saturdays was a "Do everything" day for any families in the 1960's. Laundry was full symphonic production, readying the clothes to wash, separating clothes into piles, preparing the hot water by building a fire around the wash pot to boil the white clothes and William's work over-all, mopping floors, sweeping yards, and making the monthly trip to Mobile.

Williams, Elizabeth and Shane would catch the Greyhound bus to Mobile all the way to the Bienville Square bus stop. The fare was twenty-five cents per person to take this tedious ride. All the way to the back of the bus was the first thing the driver would say to the citizens from the black community. He never said, "Good morning, hello or any other casual salutation to the black passengers; if he did it was prerequisite, by the slurs "boy" of "gal" would be his only comment."

As usual, Shane's father took her by the hand and moved she and her mother to the back of the bus, where all three were seated. As the bus moved from stop to stop picking up passengers, it filled-up fast. The driver, when he saw the bus was full and a white passenger got on, he did not moved the bus, but he sat and looked in the rear view mirror until a black person got up. William was the only black male passenger on the bus that Saturday in September 1963. He not wanting any of the women including his wife to stand or move and give their seat to a white man, so he stood and gave up his seat.

William stood and held on to one of the poles that buses had in the middle of the isles. Shane said that, "The look on his face when he moved for another white male passenger told me everything he was thinking. The look, of disgust, of humiliation and look of anger showed through."

At that very moment, Shane, who was very small in stature scooted forward in her seat, which was a struggle for her, turned around backwards and slide out of her seat and stood in front of her father, holding on to the pole and the leg of his pants as well. William stood 6'4" tall as Shane looked up at him. Shane said, "Each time she looked up at her father he looked like a giant to her." In fact, to Shane, he was a giant in life to her, period.

One of the white female passengers, said to William, "Your baby can sit down; she shouldn't be standing up."

Shane said, "No! I won't sit down! If my daddy can't sit, I not gonna sit down neither! I gonna stand with my daddy."

It was long way to Mobile starting and stopping. Even though it was tiring, she stood up with her daddy all the way on this long tedious trip.

The bus trip finally arrived at the bus stop on Bienville Square.

CHAPTER 22

Bienville Square is a remnant of Mobile's past. Bienville Square is a historical city park in the center of downtown Mobile, Alabama. Bienville Square was named for Mobile's founder Jean Baptiste Le Moyne Seur de Bienville.

Bienville Square had its beginning as a public park in 1824 as the results of a congressional act that transferred a large plot of land to the city of Mobile and designated it "Forever a park." *http://www.encyclopediaofalabama.org/face/Article.*

Today Bienville Square is used for such cultural functions: as Jazz in Bienville, Lighting of the Trees, and Kids Day in Bienville Square. As a result, of this, it is a huge change from the 1960s when only certain races of people were allowed to walk in certain areas of the park. The Bay fest Music Festival is open to all in the present day Mobile. There are no color lines, everyone comes together to enjoy the festival. It has become a crowd drawer in the South. Kids of all ages with bag lunches, toys, rides, mom's, dad's, grand's, there is a carousel of color during these time.

Bienville Square once stood as a symbol of the gentile way of life with Southern Ladies taking a Sunday afternoon stroll as they provided an array of colors with their beautiful dress and parasols. A vigilant reminder of what the South once stood for. According to the archives of the City of Mobile, "There was a good view of downtown from this park." *http://www.encyclopediaofalabama. org/face/Article. August 13, 2012*

In the center of the park presently, stands a large cast iron fountain with an Acanthus Leaf Motif. The City of Mobile added The Acanthus Leaf Motif decoration to the center of the square, in the 1890's. In addition to the fountain with the Acanthus Leaf Motif, a new bandstand darns the landscape of the park. After time and elements beat upon the fountain it had to relinquish it place to a new model same version. In 1941 the City of Mobile replaced the cast iron fountain from the Victorian Era. http://www.downtownmobile.org/ explore_attractions.html, November 2012

Bienville Park sits in the heart of downtown Mobile –right in the thick of things. As usual, in those days, there were the black and white drinking fountains. Shane said, "The fountains were not located near each other, though they were on the same side of the street, but a good three to four hundred yards apart. On the one fountain was the word "*COLORED*" written in big bold black letters. On the other fountain was the word "*WHITE*" written in bold black letters."

The fountain labeled "*Colored*" always looked like it needed cleaning. Slick green mold slime from water and sediments (who knows what kinds) engulfed the fountain. "The fountain always looked so nasty, Shane said." When she and her father and mother walked through the park on their way to the Kress or Woolworth lunch counter, she would not drink water out of the fountain even though she was so thirsty she could have drunk Mobile Bay, but refused to drink from the filthy fountain."

The other fountain labeled "White" was clean and sparkly each time she went to town with her parents and walked through the park on their way to Kress or Woolworth. There was no slime, slick mold or green stuff engulfing the fountain. Shane said, "She always wondered why the difference in the cleanest of the fountain." She would question her parents about the drinking fountain, but never got an answer that satisfied her curiosity.

In an attempt to give a logical answer to her questions about the difference in the two fountains, her parents told her that, "The black citizens were not allowed to drink from the same fountain as the white citizens." Shane was so young at that time nine or ten years old, she could not fully understand why this was so. Shane carried this question around within her mind and it became a raw open-wound, because, it was never answered.

Shane told me that, "Walking down the street in Bienville Square was a very telling journey, as they passed, white people walking in the park, her father would move here to the grass and let them pass." Shane asked her father, "Why do I always have to move daddy? Why can't the other people move sometimes?" Shane was and is a natural "Smiler." She said, "When she and her parents passed people in the square, she would wave and smile and they only threw their heads up in the air and looked the other way." Actions of other human beings, has a negative effect on children; and these actions had a negative effect on Shane.

With so many questions swirling around in her mind, Shane said, "She though like any child would, why don't white people like me or my daddy and mamma? We never did anything to them; they don't even know us. What is the difference since her parents instilled in their minds that God made and loves everybody?"

Shane said the question she put her daddy was, "Ain't we part of everybody, daddy?"

This particular Saturday in June 1963, Shane was thirsty, so it was and so happened that as their journey took them past the fountain that had *"White"* on it she stopped and turned on the water and tried to drink. William grabbed Shane by the back of her shirt and pulled her away from the fountain.

Shane went screaming and trying to pull away. "I want to get water from the clean fountain daddy, she said." William told her, "You can't drink from there, I told you that already." Shane responded, "Why? Why? this one is clean." William insistently said, "Because it is not for black folks Shane."

Shane created a scene on the street, for all on-lookers to see, both white and black. Her father continued to guide her away from the fountain.

Shane said, "She noticed as she was being pulled along that, the black people just stood in a fossilized manner and looked terrified, she said, "I always wondered why? The white folk standing there had looks of anger and disgust on their faces."

Shane said, "With her daddy pulling her along, she never got to drink from the fountain labeled "White", and she refused to drink from the fountain labeled "Colored", because of the condition it was in. It did not look fit for human consumption."

Shane said, "With her refusal to drink from the dirty fountain, she had to wait until they reached the Kress Lunch Counter, their first stop on their shopping trip, to have a glass of water. The back of Kress was the only part of the store accessible to blacks and there was a black lunch counter there. Shane finally got the drink of water, and it was out of a clean glass."

Kress lunch counter had a very sweet person, a Waitress named Mary, who worked there. Mary smiled and spoke kindly to everyone. Shane said, "She was her favorite person to see when she went to Kress. Mary always gave her an extra dill pickle with her Tuna Salad Sandwich, because she knew Shane loved them." The lunch counter extended all the way across one side of the store. It was partly in the black section and partly in the white. Shane said she noticed that, "Mary had to work both the white and black sections of the counter, but the blacks were not allowed to sit in the white section, but Mary could serve the white customers."

Kress and Woolworth the "It" place.

CHAPTER 23

Kress and Woolworth in Mobile, Alabama was "It" in the early 1960's as far as shopping was concerned for the Negro population in the whole of Mobile County. There was no such thing as going to a Department Store to shop for anything. Shane said she felt that, "Kress and Woolworth made sure that they were well stocked to make it a one-stop-shop for the black citizens of Mobile County." *University of South Alabama, McCall Library.*

Collections.alabamamosiac.org

Naturally, the merchandise was not of the same "fine quality" that was offered in the department stores. Shane said she asked her mother, "Why can't we go in the stores with the pretty things mama, we always have to go to the same stores every time we come to town." Shane said, "Her mother struggled to answer her question, and said, "Shane we have talked to you about this before, your father and I, those stores are not for people in the black race; therefore, they are not allowed to shop in them."

Shane said, "Kress and Woolworth were in the heart of downtown Mobile. Actually, it was right off of Bienville Square within a one or two block walking distance. The store was a "hot" spot for the black population of Mobile County. Saturday shopping was the "thing" in the 1960's; no one shopped during the week. Families would shop after they got paid each week. At that time, there were no Credit Cards, Debit Cards, or Checking Accounts at least; they were not known, of in the black community anyway kind of like pantyhose, unknown at that time. It was strictly a cash and carry deal with any purchases made by black customers."

Shane said, "When you walked in the store it did not need a sign "***White Only***" it was there in the actions of the people, the looks, the scoffs that could be seen from across the room from the white side of the store. The atmosphere created in the room from these looks and scoffs gave an un-welcome feeling to the entire store, especially if you were black or not of the white race."

Naturally, the socio-economic statuses at that time dictated a large portion of their lives including what one could or could not afford. There was always something a family would need, if it wasn't anything but needle and thread, so they went to downtown Mobile.

Lunch counters in the 1960's were very popular and the only sit-down meal that the Negro had the opportunity to partake of, unless it was a black-owned establishment or your home. However, not many black-owned restaurants were in existence in Mobile County at this time.

It was like an exodus when going from Chunchula to Mobile and back. There was always a feeling of being in a prison or some confined area inside the city limits. Going back home felt like freedom again, if you can imagine, at this point, you just never knew what to expect or what might happen when you were away from the sanctum of those walls at home or at least on familiar ground.

The journey to and from the city was just as startling as the journey to freedom from slavery.

CHAPTER 24

Exodus to and from freedom was a startling journey. It was amazing the evolution of the purpose, plan and plot of the Ku Klux Klan. It was a well-crafted plan. That plan grew-up like a jimsonweed, bitter and lacking in the ability to fit into society in a positive manner. On this wise, more lines with an unwanted storm attached to it came through leaving behind a wake of destruction, pain and heartache with fear as a "vanguard" before and after. This behavior of the Klan was at most reproachable. Subsequently, like all plans the Ku Klux Klan knew their nefarious scheme would not last long, it would be another hit and run scheme.

The chief tenant of the Ku Klux Klan became the black race and their rights as humans. They had no rights in the view of the Klan. The rights of the black race as an exodus; that exodus begin in the 15th century one exodus from freedom and one exodus back to freedom. www.bbc.co.uk/history/british/abolition/africa_article_01.shtml, *November 25, 2012*

Humans all have a certain amount of stewardship to one another. This is a moral stewardship to do right as much as is possible. In reference to Spiritual stewardship, all humans are part of one another in a spiritual aspect.

We are all children of God; Economic Stewardship is the well-being of the next human is our responsibility; when one person does well, so it is with everyone else humans cannot make it in the world by themselves economically. Lawful Stewardship is one that all humans have to partake. There are laws to abide by, laws of God and laws of man. The two should not conflict. *www.dictionary.com*

If we as, human beings, are doing what is lawful by God's law, then we would not have any problems with the laws of man. Therefore, whether, the stewardship is moral, spiritual, economic, or lawful, all humans have commonalities, a common ground. Ecclesiastics 4:12 "A three strand cord is not easily broken." The Bible, The Constitution, and The Emancipation Proclamation weave together a strong three-strand cord for rights and justice for all.

Not matter how many people are striving to do what is right there are always those exceptions to that rule, whether it is economically, lawfully, socially, or spiritually, they will do what is best for them and not consider or care about others in their areas of jurisdiction.

For example, as it was with several members of the Chunchula and Georgetown communities, who were known as the notorious "Uncle Toms."

There is no recognition of any Spiritual, Spiritual, Moral, or Economic Stewardship with some people no matter the importance of the neighbors or community relations.

Uncle Toms can exist anywhere at any level of human existence, so it was in Chunchula.

CHAPTER 25

Uncle Toms exist in all races. So, then you always had those that was guilty of being an Uncle Tom in the black race. "Liza Mae Watson was a female Uncle Tom, at least, that is how Shane said her mother and father William and Elizabeth described her." She told everything she knew.

She was a virtual information piece for the family she worked for, the Eatons. Ms. Liza Mae had a husband Ned, but no one hardly ever saw him, because, she was the head of the household and everything else. Shane said, "She didn't associate with blacks in the community, she stayed to herself and would not allow her husband to associate with anyone, even though he wanted to."

"Everyday there is a chance to do some of what you want so, "He would associate with everyone during the early morning hours and mid-day hours when she was not at home. But later in the afternoon as dusk begin to gather, Mr. Blue (Ned) made sure he back home, before she came from work."

Shane said, "She always thought it strange his wife would not allow him to talk with anyone. Poor Mr. Ned, he always looked so pitiful sitting on their porch when the world and neighbors passed him by."

Shane said, "He must have been sick, she didn't remember him ever working. No one, really liked Ms. Liza Mae, because they knew she was a female Uncle Tom." She was like some of the African's that sold their fellow countrymen into slavery."

Her working for the family in Georgetown seemed to give her a sense of polarization.

Liza Mae Norton and her husband Ned lived in the small town of Chunchula, Alabama during the 1960's. She built a house, on what was call "The Hill." To say Ms. Liza Mae was strange or weird would just be putting it mildly. The neighborhood labeled her a "Female Uncle Tom" – she reported on everyone to the people she worked for in Georgetown. The people/citizens in the community had to be careful what they said around her.

Ms. Liza Mae seemed to have her loyalties misplaced, not necessarily to any particular race, but to herself and her respect for who she was and her dignity as one of the members of the black community.

Shane said, "She always wondered as a child, if she was ashamed of being black, or was she afraid because she was black and thought that her friendliness with the white neighborhood would keep her safe?" She did not communicate or associate with anyone in the black community – she stood aloof of everyone else.

Ms. Liza Mae's husband was name Ned; however, everyone called him "Blue" because his lips looked like they were "Blue" even though he was as dark as a moonless night in the dead of winter. Mr. Blue was a little different from Ms. Liza Mae, his wife. He was friendly, but only, when she was not around. Ms. Liza Mae had him "hen pecked." At least, this is how it was referred to then, in the South. He acted as if he was afraid of her – draw your own conclusions on that one."

Ms. Liza Mae worked in the Georgetown community (the white section) in a couple of families homes as their housekeeper. Anything that went on in the black neighborhood, she carried it to the white neighborhood.

Shane said, "Her mother Elizabeth said, "A dog that will bring a bone, will also carry a bone."

Shane said, "She didn't understand the concept as a child, but as she grew and observed the people and surrounding around her she finally came to understand what her mother Elizabeth meant."

Ms. Liza Mae carried news of what the people in the black neighborhood did, and she bought back fabricated stories and well wishes from the white neighborhood. The fabricated stories and well-wishes that the white community sent back to the black community, by Ms. Liza Mae, were seen by the black neighbors as being falsely elusive and deceptive. The more time passed as the 1960's Civil Rights Era grew in intensity, the less the citizens of the black community would say around Ms. Liza Mae.

The lines were drawn. Children always see situations in life different from adults. A child's analysis of situations and events are, seen at their clearest. Children are innocent beings, with clearer instincts or visions than adults concerning what feels good or bad about people. Their instincts about good and evil are right on cue.

Children do not have any reason to be vindictive in the 1960's concerning race. Everybody knew what race they were in and their color. There were times when black children and white children played together before the Civil Rights Movement was full-blown; but, even then, there were not that many times, just occasionally. At this point, there were no mentions of skin color or race. Children really did not notice race or skin color at least, not the ones that Shane and her sibling played with. Keep in mind, as this story unfolds, that there are always exceptions to every story, events or situations.

Ms. Liza Mae, eventually became an outcast because of her propensity to "wag" her tongue about thing that were none of her business or anyone else's with whom she chose to talk. She seemed so enamored with the people she worked for that the fact eluded her that the information that she was taking to them played right into what they wanted to know about what was "going on" in the black neighborhood. Therefore, their actions labeled them as being, either members of the Ku Klux Klan or they were adherents, of the ideology of the Ku Klux Klan.

Ms. Liza Mae stayed labeled a female "Uncle Tom" for the rest of her life by the people of the Georgetown and Chunchula neighborhoods, both black and white. Even the citizens of the white community recognized here lack of loyalty to herself and her race. However, loyalty to self is uttermost important; loyalty to neighbors is important as long as it is not misplaced or abused.

Thereby, trust is fragile as fine China. Therefore, trust should be held, in highest of regard and with the uttermost care by and of your friends and neighbors. This is a good description of what the question of "Who is my neighbor?"

There were your Liza Mae's in the community and then there were the people like O'Man Henry in the community, another Uncle Tom.

CHAPTER 26

O'Man Henry was another interesting character in the neighborhood. At best, he was almost an anomaly of strangeness.

The Washington family had a beautiful grey dog that was as big as a St. Bernard. The family called this big beautiful steel grey dog "Jake." Jake was no ordinary run-of-the-mill-mutt from the street. William said, "He was part Shepherd and part wolf. He was very special." Indeed, he was, he was just like a protective brother. Jake was trustworthy and dependable.

Shane said, "Everyone lived in her neighborhood lived in normal looking houses. People of both races that lived in both the black and white neighborhoods had normal looking houses, except O'Man Henry, in particular who on the other hand, lived in a little cabin on what is now known as John Shinn Road." The cabin he lived in was right out of the 1870's. It was made of logs and plank that looked so strange to Shane and her sibling. It was dark and eerie, like O'Man Henry. The area around where he lived was deserted and dark. To the Washington family and other children of the neighborhood the cabin and the surrounding woods just the look of the place was scary enough without adding him into the mix."

Shane said, "His legs were full of sores; he kept them wrapped with white rags at all times; he was a thief; and he could not be trusted. He would sell his soul for a dime or a favor."

Shane said, Her Father, William, told them that O'Man Henry stole Jake, the Washington's family dog and pinned him up in a box behind his house; the children would hear Jake, but could never see him."

There was no mistaking Jake's bark. It sounded like thunder.

William told his children, "To stay away from O'Man Henry because he was dangerous and very hateful and would not think twice about hurting them. You see, O'Man Henry kept a shotgun with him at all times and would shoot if you got too close."

Shane continued to say, "He was another Uncle Tom. Oh, not to the Ku Klux Klan necessarily, but to anyone; they could be polka dot in color, he didn't care. If he had information that he thought he could place a monetary value on, he sold it to the highest bidder. The Ku Klux Klan knew this, so, they used this to their advantage. He kept an open line of information going out about what was going on in the black neighborhood, all he didn't know to be a fact; he would make him up some facts to fit the supply of information need."

Any person with these types, of characteristics are like ticking time bombs, they are dangerous and could go off at any time.

A ticking time bomb was a good description of O'Man Henry. O'Man Henry was wired to go off whenever that "need of information" button was pushed. Bombs are dangerous and destroy everything around them, as did the information line that was open between O'Man Henry and the others, whomever they might be– words can destroy, whether they are true or not.

Unfortunately, there are people of all kinds in every race with these types of characteristics. He might-as-well- been a Ku Klux Klan, he seemed to hate the citizens of the black community as much as the Klan did. Shane asked, "When do we know who we are or what we stand for? Do we have any morals or love of fellowman?"

On the other hand, there were citizens who fell as direct victims of this hate and discord that hung so heavily over the two communities because of these active Uncle Tom's with their information feeder lines.

But then again, victims of any hate and racial act could come from either male or female in the neighborhood.

Ms. Annie was one example of an individual citizen being victimized by racially biased employers.

CHAPTER 27

Not all the black citizens lived out in what was known as Georgetown. Some of the black citizen lived down in the City of Chunchula near Highway 45. There were quite a few families in one centralized area in Chunchula, kind of on a hill.

On this hill was a sweet widowed elderly lady (at least she seemed that way to a 10 year old girl) approximately fifty-five years old named Ms. Annie. She was all sugar.

Ms. Annie was a soul of kindness to her fellowman. Ms. Annie wore her kindness like a well-fitted garment. No matter who came her door she was kind to them. She would feed anyone or try to help them anyway she could.

Ms. Annie was very short in statue, light skinned and wore glasses; she did not smile a lot, but she had the heart of a saint. She would cook for the neighbors during times of illness, death, or even hard times. Like any other neighbor, she was willing to share.

Prior to the rumble, all the neighbors seemed to get along okay for a while in both neighborhoods, white and black. However after the rumble started attitudes tended toward change, especially in the white neighborhoods. This started in 1962. Every day, there was some encounter between blacks and whites; words or looks of dislike and annoyance were exchanged; but, no one had fought or had any physical contact up to this point, yet; not that there weren't causes or close calls.

Everyone seemed to hold back and continue to let incidents pass. Tension was building like a volcano; anyone could see it. The air was so thick it was like black ash from a volcano, thick enough to cut with a knife. As time passed, the name-calling got worse. The word "Nigger" was used more each day; even by the white people, who had been before, more than pleasant.

The first cross-burned, in North Mobile, was in the front yard of a black woman. The Ku Klux Klan used her as an example to get their message across to the black citizens in both the Georgetown and the Chunchula communities.

Shane said her parents told she and her sibling that the message seemed to say to all the people of the Negro race and any supporters of the negro race that, "You have no rights and you have a place, so stay in it, or you will suffer the penalty."

Ms. Annie worked for several of the white families in Chunchula; the Jacksons and the Mason's, as their housekeeper. These two families had always been nice and helpful. The rumbled seemed to change their attitudes though. Ms. Annie said, "The first morning she remembered their attitudes being different was in June of 1962. She arrived at work as usual and attempted as always before to go in the sliding door to the den. She was met at the sliding doors by Ms. Mason, who she worked for on Monday and Tuesday each week."

Ms. Mason, without mentioning her name as before, said to her, "I want you to come around to the back door from now on." Ms. Annie thought this was strange for Ms. Mason but she didn't comment, just said, "Okay, Julia, I will." Ms. Mason commented at that point, "Call me Ms. Mason from now on, not Julia."

Could her kindness in the pass have been a mask for evil?

On Thursday and Friday, Ms. Annie worked for the Jackson's. She met the same kind of attitude. Ms. Jackson met her at the den door and told her the same as Ms. Mason, "Come through the back door and call me Mrs. Jackson from now on, and not Mary." Ms. Annie as usual, said, Okay.

Could her kindness in the pass have been a mask for evil?

Ms. Annie was always one to be outspoken and if you wanted a fight; she would give you one. Not that she was violent, but she would stand her ground and stand up for her rights whether you were black or white, she did not care about color. Because, she was a soul of kindness did not mean she would let anyone just walk over her whether it was in their words or by their actions.

The second week, of this change in treatment, bought the question to the forefront. Ms. Annie asked both Ms. Mason and Ms. Jackson, "What have I done and why have the tones in your voices changed toward me and your treatment of me as well? Did I do something that I am not aware of?" No, Annie was the response, "Our husbands, "Says you are not one of us and you need to stay in your place that a "Nigga" is supposed to stay in." Ms. Annie said to them, "My name is Annie Young and not "Nigga" and furthermore, I do not appreciate being called "Nigga, either."

Usually, people fear what they do not understand, especially since Ms. Annie stopped talking to Ms. Mason and Ms. Jackson when she went to work. She said, "They watched her every move as if she was a common thief, when all the years before, she went about the daily chores unnoticed by these families as far as treating her as if they thought she might take some precious belonging of theirs."

Shane said Ms. Annie said, "They both seemed pleased with her work before."

Each week these families seemed to try to provoke some reaction from Ms. Annie, by making negative statements and using derogatory language. They got a reaction from Ms. Annie that anyone would have when someone compromises your dignity. They will speak out. This reaction to the Masons and Jacksons was a "Nigga getting out of their place."

A point well taken, one night in early July 1962 a night already sweltering with heat, to make a point to the black community, a cross was burned in Ms. Annie front yard. Ms. Annie had gone to bed at 11:00 p.m., as she did each night. The crackling sound of wood when being burned and the bright light outside of her bedroom window, awaken her a few minutes later.

There was no electricity and streetlights in the black neighborhoods in the rural community at that time, anyway. She quickly got up out of bed and looked out of the window. There in her front yard stood a burning cross, red and blue flames were shooting out from the cross and sparks were flying everywhere. A very dangerous situation at best, her house was wood framed. The cross was standing close to the house and as well as close to her flowers and Rose bushes, the setting for a small inferno in a dry already heated environment.

Ms. Annie, of course, feared for her life. She did not know if her house would be next or if the assailants were still in her yard waiting for her to run out of the house. Darkness engulfed the rural area in North Mobile County at night. In fact, she did not know what to think or what to do.

She told Elizabeth, that, "Thoughts and questions ran through her mind, who would do this cruel and frightening thing?"

Even though Ms. Annie's house stood away from the other houses in the neighborhood, danger loomed everywhere. The neighbors, when seeing the fire naturally rushed out and started trying to get the fire under control. People in the rural areas always kept several fifty- gallon drums of rainwater sitting nearby for washing clothes and cleaning their houses and other necessities. The men in the neighborhood finally put the cross out and saturated the ground around her house, as well as, the outside of her house around her house well with water to prevent a loose spark from starting up some other place near her home.

With this unexpected event, it bought even more fear in the black neighborhoods. This sudden change in the neighbor's attitudes was surprisingly enough without burning the cross.

"Strategy Time."

Therefore, Mrs. Annie needed a plan to protect herself and to save her income until she could see a little further down the road, as the saying goes.

Shane said, "This reminded her of a historical account of the fight for the Republic of Texas." Sam Houston led his army in a fast-paced flight as Sana Anna marched in pursuit. His followers thought that he was a coward and was running away, but this was not the case. Sam Houston led the army from Texas to the place they would turn a fight at the Bay of Jacinto on March 13, 1836. http://www.history.com/this-day-in-history/houston-retreats-from-santa-annas-army January 23, 2013

The black community in both small towns feared for their lives and the lives of their children. In the face of this kind of danger, they ran and stayed out of sight, at night and were careful during the day about what they said around what they called the "white folks."

The white community (not all) seemed to bask in the sudden slavery-time recognition. The black men of the community feared not for their lives only; but, also the lives of their wives, children, and the elderly.

Shane said, "Her father told them, she and her siblings, that a man will do anything to keep his family safe including take racial abuse being called a nigga, boy, hey you, or any other ugly words that can describe the distasteful feelings of one race of people for another."

Ms. Annie took the same type of abuse because she needed to work like the rest of the black community. The abuse heaped upon her was not quite as bad from Ms. Mason and Ms. Jackson during the day. The abuse that came from them when they were there with her in the daytime was that, of non-recognition of her presence as a human being, but like an object. They did not call her by name just spoke to her in a semi-rude tones.

On the other hand, when their husbands arrived home from work, the abuse went to the next level using the same ugly abusive language their husbands did, throwing around the word "Nigga". Shane recalls Ms. Annie's frequent visits to their home and she would hear Ms. Annie describing how bad it had gotten in the black community, in Chunchula.

Even when the Washington children went to the corner store , it was known as Sam's Store, the comments to she and her siblings or any other blacks in the community was, "Whata ya want Nigga? Shane said, "She could not even imagine how Ms. Annie and other adults felt because she was a child; but, she knew how she felt."

Shane said," She was scared most, of the time to the point of having nose-bleeds. She would have to sleep with her mother and father at night. The nose bleeds were bad and the pressure was unbearable, especially for a child of 10 years of age."

Shane and her siblings feared for their parents as well as themselves. For a while, Shane said, "She and her brothers and sisters were stopped from walking to the corner store in Georgetown. They went to that one because it was two miles away. The one in Chunchula was five miles away. This store was where the verbal abuse was heaped upon them. The transportation used was feet and legs. Therefore, she and her siblings went to the one that posed the least resistance distance wise.

Ms. Annie finally left the Mason's and Jackson's home. Her strategy had worked. She kept backing up until she had her had her hand out of what Shane said her mother always said, "Keep your peace until you get your hand out of the Lion's mouth." Shane said she saw Ms. Annie as a "female Sam Houston turning to fight."

She had another offer of a housekeeping position in a small town about seventeen miles from Chunchula called Eight Mile. The new employers that she worked for was Dan and Naomi Martin. The Martin's had two children, one six year old girl, Sally and a ten years old boy, Pete.

The Martin children loved Ms. Annie, as they called her. Therefore, Mr. and Mrs. Martin liked Ms. Annie. The Martins, according to Ms. Annie,

"Were strong in their beliefs about race. They would not let fear cause them to mistreat another human being." Some people always know the meaning of "Who is your neighbor."

As a result, Ms. Annie stayed with the Martin's for five years until she decided to retire and stay home to help raise her granddaughter, Belinda Washington, Shane oldest brother's James daughter. James had a daughter by Margret Young, Ms. Annie's daughter. During the interim before her retirement from working for the Martin's, she was like a member of the Martin family, coming a going each day.

Ms. Annie went in and out of any door in the Martin's home she wanted to; in addition to her other household duties, she had charge of their two children. She raised Sally and Pete for five years and was a positive influence on their lives. She talked with them about many subjects during her tenure at the Martin's, including the issues of race and issues with the Ku Klux Klan.

The Martins taught their children, Sally and Pete about color, race and difference in people, which there was no difference, only a pigmentation of the skin, because God made everyone and loves everyone; God is no respecter of person.

Mr. and Mrs. Martin was the same every time anyone saw them after Ms. Annie left their employment. Anywhere they saw Ms. Annie or anyone else in the black community; they were always respectful and kind.

Shane said, her mother comments about the Martins was, "For a couple so young they were strong and did not let themselves be swayed about color, rights, justice, or equality for their fellowman, black or white. Their belief was that God made everyone and color does not matter, but what matters is the character of the person."

As Shane said to me, "The Martins were the start of the new generation of Americans that did not adhere to that "old school" of thinking, but was the new generation on the horizon of the new America and their desire for unity and togetherness."

Indeed, they believed that, everyone made up that "We" that was spoken of in the United States Constitution. As for the Mason's and Jackson's, as time progressed, their attitudes mirrored the Ku Klux Klan whether they agreed with them because, of fear or because they had the same ideology. No matter the reason, they did not want to be considered "outcast" among their race.

Remarkably, after the Civil Rights Movement grew and begin to bring about positive change, for the black race and equal rights and justice begun to be realized; the Mason's and Jackson's tried to mix and mingle with the black community again, but was unsuccessful in their attempts. Not even one black person would agree to be their Maid; therefore, they had no choice but to hire a White Maid, for more money and less work. They were the outcast now among the black community as well as the white community. Their own race turned their backs on them as well. There were always those among the white community that stayed neutral. The tables do turn do not they?

Shane said that, "There is a margin of wisdom in being neutral as some of the white community was; they had no comments. Furthermore, a reasonable thinking person would know that nothing remains the same; it was bound to change no matter how long it took. Sometimes our tongues can hem us in and makes us more of a "slave" to our own words and actions than any whip ever can."

There were many kinds of lines during these dark days whether they were social, emotional, physical or economic, which also proved to be very true, with the lines that were drawn in the road between Highway 45 and Lott Road on what was and is still known as Georgetown/Chunchula Road.

Lines in a road should not denote a territorial ideology with racial undertones.

CHAPTER 28

Hence, lines are common on a highway or a road. They usually divide the right side of the road from the left so that traffic will not collide. They also define where a driver should or should not drive. The lines in this account are not to define where cars are to drive to prevent incidents or accident. The lines in the road in this story were of a racially biased nature and showed a clearly segregated mentality of the artist.

As the Civil Right Movement progressed, so did the aggressiveness of the Ku Klux Klan.

Shane said, "Early morning, August 1962 William Washington, Jr. discover three lines on the paved road (known as Georgetown-Chunchula Road) a quarter mile beyond the Washington family's old home place. These lines clearly symbolized where the black neighborhood ended and the white neighborhood begun."

Shane told me her father William said that, "The sunshine glistering on the painted road, bought to his mind that it might have been a Black Diamondback Rattlesnake glistering in the early morning sun as he slowly made its way across the rough highway. However, this was not the case, as he grew near to the glistering he realized that it was not a Black Diamondback Rattler but a black line painted with paint that glistened. Being prepared was always a good idea in the 1960s with the danger of animals like foxes, bobcats, or black panthers that lurked in the thickets just out of sight. William had either his shotgun or his big hickory stick that he fashioned into a walking stick/weapon. After he got nearer, he was prepared to destroy the head of the rattler's, which would not have been hard. Shane said that her father told them that snakes could not jump in a curl on a rough highway, so the danger was at a minimum as long as he kept a respectable distance."

The morning was hot and sticky as any August morning in the South is. But, more than one kind of heat was in the environment that morning; he grew very angry at what he saw and read."

Times before when the road was paved it seemed so shallow that it would not hold up under the traffic, which was minimal at best. When walking on the road, the sound that footsteps would make made it sound, as if, the road was paved over an empty-drum. Even after the county finally upgraded the paving, looking at the road still spoke the ugliness and division of the racial lines painted there. Thus reinforcing the mental lines painted in the blacks citizens minds as well as some of the white citizen's minds.

The paved roads at that time, was not as smooth as they are today. It seemed to be no more than rocks and pebbles engrained in black tar. The lines that were drawn were very evident, even before you reached them. The lines glistened in the sun light and the moon light like light when it bounces off water on a sunny day or sparkled on a full-moon-lite night.

The paint used, was permanent in nature. Shane said, "She never knew what kind of paint it was and what the mixture they used. She asked her father and he just was not sure at that time either."

So distributing were these lines that William did not allow his children to go near them for a while. The section on the road where the three lines were painted was a wooded area that could have served as a good hiding place for any assailant, man or beast.

Lines drawn in the sand were to play childish games to Shane and her siblings. The lines they drew were to play hopscotch or shoot marbles. At first, the lines drawn in the highway were odd, at the first viewing, these lines had no significance to Shane and her sibling, but it did to her parents and other parents that lived in the Georgetown community, the black community anyway.

The reasoning and significance behind the lines became clearer after a short period-of-time. The lines in and of themselves were depraved enough but what was written on both sides of the lines proved to be extremely frightening and even more disturbing. Before it had only been mental lines and vocal lines from numbers of volatile and unpredictable people, using ugly language, innuendoes, and distasteful looks upon contact. As it would have it, these lines had changed the level of the playing field.

Shane said, "She was at the point in her life that she could read well. Naturally, with her curious nature and taste for the unusual, she of course, had to see. Accompanied by her siblings (Dawn, Sharon, Chester, Michael and Elijah); they walked with intense feelings of fright stabbing at the pit of their stomachs, up the highway they went to where the lines were painted, to look at what her father told them, not to go and see."

Shane said, "What they saw there in the road was a black line, a white line and a red line all painted very neat and straight. On the side where the Ku Klux Klan decided the black neighborhood began the word "**NIGGER**" was painted in big bold black letters. On the side as you entered where the Ku Klux Klan decided the white neighborhood began, was painted the word in big bold white letters "**WHITE**" with the wide red strip painted close to the white line." (picture of the road with the stripes drawn placed here.)

Photo 1
Old road in 1960s and 1970s lines were drawn Black, White and Red.

Photographer: Mr. Nasrullah Aziz, Professor of Mathematics,
Alabama School of Mathematics and Science, January 15, 2013.

Photo 2

Road as it appears today, 2013. This picture is taken of highway (road) with author, Carlotta Maria Shinn Russell pointing to the spot where the lines were painted, as showed her by Shane Washington, and where the lines would be today, if the highway had not been resurfaced. See Photo 1, for the lines, as they were painted in June 1963, black, red and white.

Photographer: Mr. Nasrullah Aziz, January 15, 2013.

Shane continued to say that, "She and her sibling returned home to find their father waiting, because they had disobeyed his warning. After the appropriate lecture and stern warning of punishment, Shane said, "She and her siblings questioned their parents about the meaning of the red line. Their response to them was simple and to the point. William and Elizabeth said to their children, "The red line means that they consider themselves doing Christ a favor by getting rid of people of color or the black race."

Shane said that, "By this juncture in their lives and the core of the Civil Rights Movement as an ongoing day-to-day event; she and her sibling knew the meaning of the racial slurs that the Ku Klux Klan threw at them, their neighbors and those they thought were "helpers" of the black race. They too would be subject to the same type of cruelty."

Shane said, "After a few weeks, with those emotions that ran so high at the event and appearing of those lines, the Washington children took their usual walk to the corner store. They had to cross the lines in the road going and coming from the little country store that was about two miles from their home. As they walked through the white neighborhood there were on the faces: frowns, looks of disgust, scoffs, racial slurs, murmuring under the breath, and name-calling. But no one attempted to do any physical harm to them, Tank and his brother Jessie, were thought of by the Washington children as the "Fido" team was in their usual spot on their front porch with that bulldog on a chain."

The Washington children walked on the left side of the road going to the store and on the right side of the road returning from the store. They were told by their parents, "To tend to their own business and do not say anything to anyone except each other."

Even though the lines were there and the threat of danger loomed large, none one would bother the Washington children.

Who the artist was that painted those lines, were never known, not to the black neighborhood anyway. As usual, the Washington children had their suspicions of the identity of the painter.

The county transportation department eventually paved out those three lines in that road, but paving is a physical action. However, they could not pave out the lines in the minds or the hearts of the citizens; it is a matter of choice of each of the individuals whether they allow racial lines to be permanent fixtures in their minds and hearts. Only each of the individuals can paint out those lines and replace with the word "finally", which should pre-requisite the following nouns: justice, peace, freedom, and equality.

The racist ideology of the Ku Klux Klan is not dead yet, like the lines on the surface of Georgetown-Chunchula Road, which are below the painted surface.

Shane said, "She believes, if you scrape deep enough you will find them, timeless and in place like the ideology of the Klan, if you dig far enough that, racist ideology is still there."

Not only were lines drawn to fence in the black race but, lines were drawn for those who would help a beleaguered and persecuted people.

Besides the lines drawn for the Negro race, there were lines drawn for one of this nation's brightest stars who took a stand for equality and freedom for all people of America.

Assassination is a dreadful crime. America as a whole, faced one of the bleak's days in the history of this country since the start of the Civil War with the firing on Fort Sumter in Charleston, South Carolina, April 12, 1861. http://www.nps.gov/, October 2012

In this light, the assassination in Texas of the President of the United States in 1963, John Fitzgerald Kennedy Jr., took place during the height of the Civil Rights Movement, was one unforgettable morning that lives forever, in the memories children that were raised at this period in time

CHAPTER 29

The John F. Kennedy, Jr.'s, assassination sent shock waves through the nation and around the world.

Shane said she did not think that, "The 1960's during the Civil Rights Movement was a very ornate time in history, not a lot of flair and sparkle accompanied this period of time just pain, suffering and fear, leaving America with this period as an "unforgettable" time in the history of this country."

At the point when President Kennedy was assassinated November, 1963 Shane was still a very young girl. There are many unforgettable events and days in her life.

Unfortunately, there are those days that are unusually unforgettable like this school day. The school day on this unforgettable day started as usual for the Washington family in November 1963. **Source Kennedy Assassination**

There was nothing special about this day lunch was prepared as usual, Tuna Fish Sandwiches or Peanut Butter Sandwiches was always, the lunch of the day. Off to the school bus stop to catch the bus. The bus ride was noisy with an array of conversations going on by children of all ages and at the same time…the sound of happy children. Shane said, "They arrived at school and went through the regular duties of a school day morning.

Shane attended Rosa A Lott School, a segregated black school. It was in actually, the only black school in a very wide radius out in the rural Mobile County. All Students including Shane and her brothers and sisters rode the yellow hound to school.

Surprisingly, the school was a modern school in the 1960s and well kept. The principal, Mr. Wilson, got as much of the best for his students that he could. It was amazing that the school was so well equipped which also afforded an environment for the students that was conducive for both studying and learning, but it did.

The memories that Shane said she had of her school days were pleasant, but there were no encountering other races in an all-black school, therefore no race issue ever came up, and for that she was thankful.

However, anywhere else she went, did not offer this type of "sanctum" or that particular type of "race safe" environment.

As mid-morning approached, there began to be the sound of shuffling feet and animal-like sounds when an animal have been wounded, whimpering sounds when pain is being inflicted upon someone all coming from the hallway.

Mr. Wilson, the Principal appeared at Shane's classroom door.

Immediately, upon Mr. Wilson's arrival, he called Ms. Harris, Shane teacher, to the door. He whispered something to Ms. Harris. The look of horror, fear and complete confusion on Mrs. Harris's face put knots in Shane's stomach. Mrs. Harris walked back to the front of the class and said, "Class, John F. Kennedy, Jr., President of the United States, was just shot and killed." Shane said, "She wanted to run and hide, and other children began screaming and calling for their mothers." It seemed like it was an eternity before Ms. Harris got the students quieted down again."

Shane continued to say that, "The students did not completely settle down the remainder of the day. So many of the children's faces, had looks of an over-powering fear on them that morning, in November 1963. The atmosphere in the room immediately turned somber and grey, as the knots grew tighter in Shane's stomach. She felt as if she could not catch her breath for the longest time. Anxiety set in which took a toll on the children, when more fear is layered, upon the already unbearable fear, that is unrelentingly haunting the children because of the already present fear in their environment. She felt as if the Tank's and Jessie's of the world were everywhere."

Shane said, "She could not eat her lunch that day, it would not go down. She was even afraid to go to the bathroom by herself for fear that someone or something may be there to harm here. She wanted to go home to see if her mother was okay. She was be alone during the day when she and her siblings was away at school and their father was working in the field near her grandfather's house, William Sr. She was afraid for her mother, afraid someone would try to harm her before she and her siblings got home from school."

"Shane stayed close to Mrs. Harris the rest of the day."

"The ride back home from school on the bus that afternoon was not cheerful as the ride to school that morning. All of the children on the bus seemed to feel like Shane did. Their stomach, seem to feel, if it was tied in knots, as well. Some of the children were leaning forward holding their stomachs. Some were leaning forward with their head on their hands on the rail of the seat in front of them. There was no chatter and happy sounding voice of children just an environment of anxiety."

"Shane said, Elizabeth, her mother, was clearly upset and shaken when they got home from school, though she did her best to hide it. She was waiting for them at the bus stop, which was unusual. Her face was bleak and had an upset look about it, when ordinarily she smiled when she saw her children coming from school."

"This seemingly unsettled and evidently shaken mother did not help Shane and her siblings fears it only added additional fear to the fear already floating around. All evening, after they arrived home from school and evening chores were finished, the family listened to the news about the assassination, of the President of the United broadcasted on the battery-operated radio that sat on an old antique stand in the corner of their living room. There was a quiet about her parents that, Shane had never seen."

Shane told me her parents said, "They have just killed "one of the hopes" for the black people in this country. He was a friend to all the people in America."

Shane said, "Dealing with the knots in your stomach is like trying to unravel a knotted set of strings; it was almost impossible. There was not reasoning with the knots in the pit of her stomach and that choking and hard to breathe feeling she was having."

This long horrible night after the heartbreaking morning that President Kennedy was assassinated, the Washington family and other families in the neighborhood spent another miserable night with quiet voices and the lamp light turned low with no shadows and no noise.

Shane said, "Once again she had to sleep with her parents because of the pressure that this level of fear caused resulting in almost unstoppable nose bleeds."

There were racial biases going on across the South in all directions whether they were north, south, east or west. There is always another real life example that can be applied.

The historical account of the black basketball team in Texas paints a most vivid picture and very good example of the pressures of racism and bias that still exist at all levels.

Glory Road was very revealing in reference to the questions of race and equality during the 1960s.

CHAPTER 30

I used the story Glory Road, to emphasize the magnitude of racism in the 1960s and to accentuate the difficult times the Negro was force to endure during the Civil `Rights Movement. In the 1960's a coach had a vision that did not include color of a player's skin; rather he looked for skill, character and the quality of his player's abilities without regard to race. The story of a predominately-black team, of a community college in small town in Texas is a true story recorded in history.

Glory Road, is another example of injustice to members of the black race because of color or the perception that the black man lacked the ability to perform at a professional level. They suffered for their skills and abilities. It appeared to be a shock to the coaches, recruiters, etc. that a team of mostly black basketball players could unite and carry their team to victory. What a shocking revelation! What a dangerous revelation! To realize that the black man was a powerful force when let loose....unbounded by chains of racism, difference, and bias.

A powerful forced that changed the game of basketball forever and the perception of the black man not having the ability to play at the national level was gone. No more highly offensives terms like: coon, spics, or niggers could be wore as a label by the team members, but professional players that could think, plan, strategize, and execute a team play. http://gloryroad.utep.edu/home.aspx February 21, 2013

This was another example of power, the very thing that the Ku Klux Klan did not want the black man to have; they were treated like children in the eyes of the Ku Klux Kla. Here again, that race line existed.

In contrast, like their efforts to prevent the vote of the black man. Voting in and of itself is power, just as is knowledge. This prospect was scary. Power is a fearful thing in the hand of the wrong people which, the black race was seen as being those wrong hands of power.

The determination to keep this "child" in a permanent condition of fear for the rest of their lives was the aim of the Ku Klux Klan—with a mechanism of fear working, the black man could not concentrate too much on freedom, just staying alive. Fear is a pressure, a loose wrecking ball hanging by a weak link on a chain. Applying any amount of pressure will cause the link to break.

Metaphorically, fear is like a brick wall. Fear prevents progress. Fear is an opposing force. Fear is unhealthy for a people's social and emotional well-being. Just as it were to the basketball team's emotional health, for a while, the opposition to a mostly predominantly black team affected their ability to perform. How can you perform when you are afraid? That wall of fear can be daunting. This could not be allowed as a permanent condition for this predominately black team. For a while, the players were only existing and not living. The black players inability to perform was having an effect on the white players as well. This is always a possibility with any situation in life. All human beings are connected. Humans are either related by their bloodline, situations, events, or time. However, adding pride along with self-assurance and belief in their skills and abilities as a team, not a black team would finally in and of itself effected a change, as it did with the final line in this historical example.

In the meantime, there were other incidents taking place in Texas within this same time-frame.

Michelle Ogden, who was born, raised and educated in North View a small town outside of Denton, Texas, gave me a similar account of her family's travails and anguish because they were members of the black race.

CHAPTER 31

I spoke with Michelle Ogden who now lives in Winterville, North Carolina concerning her experience as a child living in a racially biased state.

Michelle Ogden grew up in small town outside Denton, Texas called North View. She and her family lived on the Eastside of the town "across the tracks." There were two railroads tracks that sandwiched in the town; either way, one way or the other you lived either across the railroad tracks or between the railroad tracks.

Michelle said that, "In the 1960s the black community was in a poverty condition on more than one level. There were no swimming pools, for the "colored" community, no theatres, no restaurants, and no public activities. The schools for blacks were inferior. The students that attended the black schools in North View did not have the opportunity to enjoy the privileges, of having new textbooks from which to study. The new books that they got were the hand-me-downs from the white students."

Michelle took me on a mental tour of the city of North View. The most outstanding point on this tour that stood out in my mind was the bus station. On the left was the bus station, there inside was a sign posted over a water fountain labeled "COLORED" the bathrooms had "COLORED" signs over the doors and they were in a less-kept condition than the bathrooms labeled "WHITE."

As far as food was concerned, if you went to a fast food restaurant you went to the back door to order and would get your food to go. There were no sit-down privileges to eat for black citizens.

Michelle said that, "It was a long time before the black citizens were allowed to even ride the city buses. After they were allowed to ride the city buses, they had to ride in the back of the bus, but if there were no seats on the bus, you got up and gave your seat to the white person whether they were a male or female."

Michelle said, "At that time, both her parents were fortunate enough to have jobs. She said that, "Strangely every year there was an event held that included all the black employees in their little town, here parents employers as well. The different employers, whoever they were, would give their black employees, on a day set aside each summer, a picnic. They held the yearly picnic, in a huge field, located on the outskirts of the little town of North View. The entire event had a most uncanny overtone to it. It was bizarre that this yearly meal was a meal that everyone knew that black citizens would eat at any picnic. They seem always to associate Fried Chicken with the black race in North View. Michelle said, "The meal sent this message to her as a child, "You are black." The menu included: Fried Chicken, Barbecue Ribs, Baked Beans, Macaroni and Cheese with a Tossed Salad and a Red Pop."

The employers made this their signature meal each year. The employees did not have to wonder what they would have for their food.

Michelle continued to say that, "With both her parents being blessed to work, her family had a fairly decent income. She said her mother Rachel worked for a the Williams family in North View. Her father Clyde worked at the local factory where a good number of the black men worked."

"With the different directions here parents having to go, her father decided to purchase her mother a 1962 Chevrolet Impala to drive to work. Due to the distance she had to travel, it would not allow her to walk, as many of the black Maids and other workers had to do during that time. The car was a reasonably decent one. In addition to that, her father went the opposite way in his old pick-up truck; therefore, he could not drop her mother off at work."

This car, the 1962 Chevrolet Impala did not set to well with her employer Ms. Williams. Michelle said, "Her father told she and her sisters that their mother's car seemed to Ms. Williams, her employer as if it was in better condition than hers; therefore, she had Rachel to park her car behind her house so the neighbors could not see it. Michelle said that Ms. Williams told her mother that, "Because her neighbor's perception that she had the better car would prove embarrassing to her with them thinking that her black maid had a better looking car than she did."

Those were painful years to get pass.

Michelle said, "After she got through her painful growing years and finally high school years, she graduated in May of 1964. She decided to attend college in Texas at North Texas State University, a State operated institution. In fact, "A State school was all that most black citizens were allowed to attend, or for that matter could afford in the 1960s."

Michelle said, "In August 1964, she traveled by bus to North Texas State University in Denton, Texas. On the way to college in Denton, she looked out of the window, of the bus, and there on the side of the highway nailed to a tree was a wood poster painted with the effigy of a black man hanging from a tree with a sign that said, *"The only good Nigger is a dead Nigger."* This effigy of the hanging black man painted a horrible and frightening mental picture, for a young black female leaving home for the first time."

According to the dictionary effigy is defined as, a crude figure or dummy representing a hated person or group. http://www.thefreedictionary.com/effigy February 21, 2013

Michelle said, "She was barely eighteen years of age when she left home for the first time in her life."

Michelle said that, "This was a terrifying and very unnerving scene. How can humans dislike or despise other so much? It was insulting and scary to her."

Hence, 1964, was the first year that students that attended North Texas State University were allowed to stay on campus. In Denton, as in North View, black students nor the black citizens were allowed to eat in any public places. They got their food from the back doors of food establishments and took it with them. Another example of the kind of "Back Door-ism" that was commonplace in the 1960s to the black race.

She said, "In addition to all of the culture shock that was environmentally present at that time, she had to deal with the possibility of flunking out of a class, English, of all subjects."

Michelle related to me that, "One of the English Professors at North Texas State University (whom she preferred not to name), was known by all the black students as "one" to be avoided. He made the statement at the beginning of each semester that, "He would never pass a black student."

Michelle said, "This professor never called on black students in class during an in-class discussion. He indulged in the non-recognition of people of color. This class was most important to Michelle, it carried one-third of your grade, you would never passed a test, nor would a black student ever write a "good enough" essay." She carried the fear of flunking this instructor's class with her every day, always expecting the unexpected. Ultimately, she did manage to pass the English class with a fairly decent grade."

Michelle Ogden told me that her experiences as a child, "Left lasting memories of what could have been the future of the black race had it not been for citizen that were willing to take up the fight for freedom and push until those lines began to fade and that walls of racism begin to come down. Even with the fight it left her with scars, though they healed, the memories are still there"

Just as it was in North View, Texas like incidences, were happening all over the South and other parts of the nation, whether they were before, during or after the Civil Rights Movement.

There were always spurts of Civil Right Movements no matter the geographic locale. As with the story of the Raisin in the Sun, a movie filmed in Chicago concerning the racial biases a family met in in the next community when a family tried to change their soci-economic status in life.

CHAPTER 32

I used several stories that are familiar to all citizens across America to make a point.

Even in Chicago, the North, which the movie The Raisin In The Sun , by Lorraine Hansberry, was filmed or featured, depicts one family on Chicago's south side in poverty who tried to pull themselves out after receiving a boost from the death of the family's father. Attempting to live their dream, the family purchased a house across the societal bridge from a poor black neighborhood into an all-white neighborhood. However, the neighbors did not want them to mix. http://www.timbooktu.com/orlgreen/raisin.htm February 21, 2013

http://www.biography.com/people/lorraine-hansberry February 21, 2013

This story depicts real life as it unfolded across the South and other parts of the nation.

With this purchase of a home in the white neighborhood, they had crossed a line. To prevent the mixing of people from the black race, the neighborhood took drastic measures. A buyout was the only thing to do. The neighbors pooled their money and offered the family a buy-out.

This buyout was completely unexpected by the family.

The offer made was to buy them out, was to keep them out. The neighbors offered the family a token, of pacificity that would keep them in the same poverty conditions with no change in their socio-economic status they could not improve their perception of themselves as a people of solid citizenship and as important members of the human race.

But here again, do you let yourself be railroaded, kept in a position of poverty, whether it is of location, of physical, or of mental or of emotional poverty or do you reach down and pull out that pride that is within you as an important part of the human race who have a contributable value?

As seen in the movie or read in the book, the family suffered from a poverty of spirit another form of slavery.

Even though the temptation was there to accept the buyout, they overcame their fears and the decision were made to keep the house across the societal bridge and move out of the poverty conditions they were forced to, for years to survive under, because of their overall economic status.

Desperation can cause humans to do desperate things to rise to success or improve conditions, for their families, this too, is an opposing force.

The Ku Klux Klan ideology help build this wall and the black race kept running into it.

After a while you will get tired, so what do you do? Remove the wall, cut a hole in it no matter the method of escape you will find or make a door for passage. The family moving into the white neighborhood was that door and passageway.

No buy out here, if the offer made do not better your condition, why take it or more than that, why let it be the tool used to take it from you?

So, what do you do, just give up or just give in to the pressure or intimidation?

Sometimes, we are our own worst enemy.

What a picture we draw of ourselves. An individual or race of people have to stay down or lay down before people can keep you down or walk on you. If you stumble and fall, get up and try it again, which was the end results of the family portrayed in the movie/book. Dreams of success either live or die in our mind; or in this example, within this family as a unit.

Progress, in any movement should be evident at some point. Are we as a nation making progress? Is each State looking to the future and changing those laws and situations that were or could have been some of the major players in the lines that were drawn?

Looking at the State of Alabama, where are we now?

CHAPTER 33

Where are we now?

Alabama still has a problem that sticks out like a sore thumb. The Constitution of the State of Alabama has a great amount of racist language written in it and racist laws that directly affect the citizens of Alabama, both black and white.

The Constitutional Laws, in particular, that has not been changed for more than one hundred years; especially those about race are there and can be noted as being biased. One hundred years is a long time to govern under a century of Constitutional laws that does not apply to "today."

A Constitutional Reform Committee have been formed in the State of Alabama that has undertaken this task to effect a change to the laws on the book; however, this committee is like a grinding wheel, it has many too many fights, rough edges, trenches, and broken axels to get past.

Shane's opinion, when I asked her where she thought Alabama is now in regards to the laws that require fairness, for each of their residents was.

Rhetorically she said, "Where do I think we are we now approximately forty-eight years later in the South after the Civil Rights Movement?"

"Looking forward to approximately forty years after the Civil Rights Movement, the struggle for equality, for each citizen, of the State and their abilities to make choices has not been realized in the State of Alabama, not in written form anyway."

Shane continued to say, "It took from the inception of the Civil Rights Movement in the 1960s, until the year 2000 to effect a change in the Alabama Constitution "Amendment 666." However, Amendment 666 of the Constitution did not annul the 'Article IV, Section 102' stated in the Alabama Constitution as follows "The Legislature shall never pass any law to authorize or legalize any marriage between any white person and a Negro or descendent of a Negro." **Alabama State Constitution www.al.gov**, November 25, 2012.

"Therefore, this overrides the U. S. Constitution and the Amendment that grant all men the rights to be free to choose at any level whether, they want to marry someone of a different race or not. It is like drinking water out of a fountain. There should have been no restriction at any time on: the freedom to drink water from a clean fountain, sit at a lunch counter, eat a meal anywhere one so chooses, regardless of skin color or walking down the street having to move to one side, actions like this could have gone on, for an eternity"

I asked Shane, "Are we much further today than we were forty-eight years ago?"

Shane said, "This question, I think, can be best answered by looking at our past or by finding our past."

"To answer this question we can rate ourselves on a "Race Progress Scorecard.""

CHAPTER 34

Finding our past or looking at our past, can help us to identify what the problems were and see where the disparities lie, as well as, look at what the possibilities are to learn from the past and make every effort to effect a positive change.

Why flounder in the past, trying to reinvent slavery or keep a race of people unlike yourself under bondage? The physical bondage was not there anymore, but the mental and emotional bondage are not completely gone.

So many things Shane said that, "She was told by her parents that black people could not do."

Shane said, "This was confusing to here; she did not understand the concept. Her parents, grandparents, all the adults she knew told her that God made man in his image and all races of men came from one man, Noah." The concept of all three children being born to one man was understandable, but the rest was not, at least not at ten years of age. *Genesis: 9:1: Then God blessed Noah and his sons (Ham, Shem and Japheth), saying to them, "Be fruitful and increase in number and fill the earth." Master Study Bible, King James Version of the Bible, 2001*

The lines that were drawn seemed to Shane to increase more and more; there was always something, she could not do. Shane said that, "She started to look at people with different eyes, in reference to how they might be thinking. Were they thinking about color when they saw her or just looking at her as a little girl?"

Shane said, "She felt as if she lived in another world, one world for the whites and one world for the blacks and there was no crossing the line."

Shane said, "She did not know how to put her feeling about this period of time in prospective. She talked with her mother about how she felt, but as always, her mother spoke with kindness about the race issues."

Shane said, "She realized that her mother was trying to avoid tainting her children's minds about people of other races. Even though, every effort was made to prevent the negative thought processes, it did not stop the resentment Shane and her sibling felt about the issues of race."

The seemingly adamant dislike that the white citizens and the black citizens in the Georgetown/Chunchula communities had for each other was very evident. The dislike for each other stuck out like a sore thumb and the children, like the adults they mirrored, the entire neighborhood stood behind the lines with their fists drawn ready to fight. Whether the battle fought was, of a mental, of a physical or of an emotional one. These Battle lines in Chunchula/Georgetown, were depicted by more than the lines that was drawn on the highway.

How can you see your parents and others in the neighborhood mistreated and not take their side? There is no way that those lines drawn would not have an impact on a child's thinking and feelings. These feeling grew as Shane and her siblings and other grew into young adult years on both sides of the color lines.

As the Civil Rights Movement advanced and intensified, so did the resentment of the Ku Klux Klan and their actions that spilled over and influenced more and more people around them; the lines got stronger and tension grew tighter.

Shane said, "Adulthood started with so many questions about who, you are and where is your place in this country where all men are supposed to be free to move around at their own discretion."

The March on Washington to the foot of The Lincoln Memorial led by Martin Luther King, Jr. was a defining moment in time. Dr. King, finally, clarified what that "Foot" Rosa Parks put across that color line meant when she refused to give up her seat for a white man on a bus in Montgomery, Alabama in 1959. That single step changed the world for both blacks and whites forever.

Shane said, "In 1968 she had grown into young adulthood with Segregation still nipping at her hills, she still felt trapped behind that color line."

Shane stated that, "Her mother Elizabeth told her during the critical times in the 1960s, the rest of the world, including the Northern part of America, was watching to see what actions would be taken to help eliminate this horrible injustice by a white supremacy group who did not want blacks to vote. But, the Ku Klux Klan with their efforts to prevent the black race from voting and gaining this power had carried their preventive strategy to the next level and elimination of the blacks were added to their list. This became tiring and debilitating, therefore the Negro had gone as far to their Bay of Jacinto (1856) as they were going." In history, there is the account of Sam Huston and his fight for freedom for the Republic of Texas, as he fled from his pursuer, General Santa Annas, which can be, compared or contrasted with the dilemma of the black race. http://www.history.com/this-day-in-history/houston-retreats-from-santa-annas-army August 25, 2012

Sam Houston, while being chased by Santa Annas, Mexican General, led the Mexican Army to the Bay of Jacinto, where they would turn and fight, winning their battle with minimum casualties. http://www.history.com/this-day-in-history/houston-retreats-from-santa-annas-army August 25, 2012

The black race, like Sam Huston and their Sam Houston (Martin Luther King, Jr.), for the black republic of the United States, led the Movement in a peaceful manner. Only those with vision could see what Sam Houston was doing and only those with vision could see what Martin Luther King, Jr., was doing.

The "flight rather than fight" serves a purpose until it is appropriate to turn the tables. Peace is what both of these movement leaders sought, so they followed a planned (strategy) until it accomplished their mission. Faith was what both had in the mist of all of the turmoil. No matter the size of the problem or how difficult the road to peace, Houston and King were willing to pay the price.

The Bible reminds us in Hebrews 11:1: Now, faith is the substance of things hoped for and the evidence of things not seen. The *Master Bible, King James Version, 2001*

For instance, no matter the fight or the racial biases hurled there are always those that hold to or adhere to their principles and can decide what is right or wrong using their own reasoning abilities.

Ethan Scott was one of these young people raised in Georgia during in the late 1950s and early 1960s who was exposed in a two-folded way to both sides of the coin of racism and to what was the right way to treat your fellowman.

CHAPTER 35

As the author of this book, I wanted to have more than one account of the perceptions of children during these dark years of the Civil Rights Movement. An account of what other children experienced or if they witnessed racial disparities in their neighborhoods or in the city or state of their residence.

Ethan Scott graciously agreed to give me his experiences as a child dealing with this two-sided coin. Ethan detailed this true story to me, of the events in his life as he grew from childhood to a young adult. Ethan Scott lived in Georgia in the 1950s and early 1960s. Ethan told me. "He saw many unusual events around him as a child."

Born as a native son of the State of Georgia, and as he grew his description of these facts were through, his "eyes" when he was a child. He gave me a very vivid account and of his perception as a child, the events that took place in the racially divided South in the 1950's and the 1960's in his community.

Ethan said, "Growing up in the South, in the 1950's and the 1960's placed a young white male in an all too interesting set, of circumstances. On the one hand, I learned from the pulpit on Sunday's that all men were God's children; but on the other hand, throughout the week, I received innumerable signs that people of African (black, Negro) origins were somehow in a "less – blessed" predicament. Therefore, these were mixed messages."

Ethan said, "Later, I felt that I was very fortunate to have paid much stricter attention to the material from the pulpit. In fact, the more I listened to the Preacher on Sundays and the more I read, the more racial difference in those scriptures seemed to be taken positive things of great interest far from anything like racist slurs."

Ethan gave this examples to make his point clear about how he felt about race.

Ethan said, "There was, the Syro-Phoenician Woman, the Good Samaritan, The Roman Cornelius, and others. The stories concerning them bought messages of great import, but nothing that would suggest the superiority of one group over another. So, in the long term, I believe that those young white men like myself in those not-so-far-off days were truly blessed if they were more influenced by the Pastor in this regard and loss what seemed popular in the day-to-day."

Shane said, "There were many young Ethan Scott's in the 1950's and 1960's in the white race, even in Chunchula, and as they grew, they learned from the influence of the Pastor and not listen to what mainstream society would teach them about race and bias."

Ethan Scott was one of the "helpers" not necessarily what he did physically, but what he did characteristically. He possessed the type of character that the Martins had, the family for whom Ms. Annie worked who had no preference or bias to a person because of their skin pigmentation. To stand on your principles were hard, especially in the 1960's. This is one of the strong characteristics of a helper. Knowing how to distinguish between what is right and what is wrong is a definite mark of true character for someone that believes that all humans should have the same God-given rights to freedom.

There can always be an example that can give support to a disfranchised race of people through events depicted on the website: http:/blackpast.org.

Rosewood, Florida and the tragedy that took place there is an example.

CHAPTER 36

The events in this account happened in Florida more than thirty-seven years before the Civil Rights Movement of the 1950s and 1960s took place.

The story of Rosewood is a about true events that happened approximately seventy+ years ago. Rosewood citizens suffered the same kinds of racist bias the citizens of Chunchula, Alabama suffered in the 1960s. There were many "Rosewoods" in the South in the pre-dawning and post-dawning years of the Civil Rights Era.

The freedoms granted by The United States Constitution were not realized quiet yet by citizens of either town, Chunchula, Alabama or Rosewood, Florida.

Shane said she thought of it in this way, "We were free, but we were not free. Those lines existed on more roads than in Chunchula, Alabama."

The mental lines are far worse than the physical line. The physical lines will eventually disappear with rain, time, or wear. Although the physical lines are gone by covering them with new tar and gravel or by time, the effect of the elements or the cleansing rain, which eventually washed them out the mental lines remains forever.

Bitterness and hatred of a fellowman or a race of people wrap ideas, thoughts and causes actions that should be uncommon to any man against another, no matter the race, creed, or origin of culture from which a race of people come. To have negative thoughts should not influence man's thoughts and actions about or against another human being to the point that it becomes physically and mentally destructive.

As in this historical account, the racial lines were clearly drawn. The typical black and white neighborhoods were there; it may not have been a physical line painted in the road, but the mental lines were there. Chunchula, Alabama could have been Rosewood or vice-versa.

The situation, at best was uncomfortable for both races. There are always those in the mix that does not agree with the cruelty and disrespect heaped upon another race of people. Like the point in Rosewood, so it was in Chunchula, everyone does not agree with the treatment of the other race, but who is to speak out? There was just as much danger from them as it was for the people targeted with the bias or racism.

On January 1, 1923, a Massacre was carried out in the small predominately black town called Rosewood, in Central Florida. The massacre was initiated by the rumor that a white woman, Fanny Taylor, had been sexually assaulted and beaten by a black man in her home. In a nearby community, a group of white men believing the report to be a recently escaped convict named Jessie Hunter, along with Aaron Carrier and Sam Carter two other males who were believed to be accomplices. The suspect Aaron Carrier was captured put in jail and hung. Carrier was suspected of hiding Hunter in his home in Rosewood. A mob assembled to capture the man.

Prior to this event, a series of incidents had stirred racial tension within Rosewood. During the previous winter in1922, a white School Teacher from Perry had been murdered. On New Year's Eve in 1922 there had been a Ku Klux Klan rally held in Gainesville, Florida, located not far from the little town of Rosewood. *http://www.blackpast.org/?q=aah/rosewood-massacre-1923*

The same patterns were seen in many the black communities. The ideology had been in force for years. As time went on, the momentum escalated a process that kept growing until it became a destructive force in-and-of-itself. That force along with the ideology destroyed many lives and instilled enormous amounts of fear into the black communities as well as the white communities.

As Langston Hughes said, "The Negro, humble, docile, and kind; beware, the day they change their minds." The Negro mind-change started to in the late 1950's and early1960's. A new generation emerged with a leader that was not afraid to step-up-to the plate; thinking of it in this light then, he too was afraid like everyone else, which brings about another paradox.

Shane said to me that she though that, "The fear that Dr. King had was that, if someone did not take a stand, the plight of the minority races no matter who they were would be sealed forever. This paradox, of fear was an emotional fear of one who suffers because of the inequality and lack of justice for a race of people."

The Klan treated the Negro as if they looked at them as if they were chickens hiding from a hawk—this proved not to be so. This humble, docile sweet and kind Negro race did change their mind. They fought back in a manner that took the entire nation by surprise; they took a peaceful stance to the war for freedom this time; no guns, no violence, but a peaceful ideology, an ideology opposite from what the Klan had purported all the years before.

The Negro like the oak tree, the branches may break and fall, but the root and base of the oak is still strong and well rooted; even when there is destruction within a race of people, the race like the oak tree, will survive. The roots are always there.

The Negro had done their duty for King and Country and freedom was still not theirs to enjoy and possess without having to pay a further price.

Shane said that, "She saw Martin Luther King, Jr., as a leader who had a passion for equality and justice for everyone not just the black man; he cared about all peoples. Dr. King's quest for true freedom, justice and equality was a tireless effort. In this case, this fight was for the black man, because the black race was the main-focus, the target, for the inequality and injustice hurled at them by the Ku Klux Klan and those that followed or practiced their ideology."

Therefore, freedom, equality and justice, these are rights due every human to live and enjoy those laws, which provided freedom to live in the greatest nation on earth. These are such freedoms like, the rights to vote and freedoms to choose and the rights to move around in this land without fear of assault.

These were some of the freedoms set in motion, by the Forefathers of this nation. People of the black race, was seen as property and not human beings, who did not deserve those freedoms. One human cannot and should not own another, lawfully or morally.

Dreams can often become reality if the dream of one man is powerful enough. Dr. Martin Luther King, Jr. was such a man with such a dream.

CHAPTER 37

One man with a dream, The Dream of Martin Luther King, Jr., became a reality in the late 1950s and early 1960s. It only takes one human with a dream that is all-inclusive to start a movement that took a nation in a positive direction; it took sacrifice and change to get us there.

Martin Luther King, Jr. was the 1960's Civil Rights Movement "Helper" and then again, he was more than a Helper. He was a charismatic leader who took up the sword and led the battle for final freedom: freedom for the black race and all those that would come hereafter, of a minority status in America. Now, this sword was not a weapon that would physically destroy lives, but this sword was a sword of "Peace." Dr. King, used reasonability and the law to fight for freedom promised and already written into the United States Constitution, the Emancipation Proclamation and The Holy Bible.

The fight was a long and arduous one, with many soldiers for peace falling on the battlefield on the way to complete liberty. Shane told me that, "She always wondered why Martin Luther King, Jr. would risk his life, for a fight that the black race seemed to continually lose? As well as one, that had been going on for centuries, which was not getting better no matter the amount of time passed but, rather it seemed to be going backward, or not moving at all?"

Besides, living in status quo has never been an attractive feature. When people say everything is "Okay" it is status quo is very unnerving, "If it aint broke don't fix it." When considered, the facts are that, complete freedom for the Negro was never" fixed" from the beginning; it was only fixed on paper, but not in actuality.

There has been and will always be someone that will take up the fight, for Freedom and lead the march for those that are less fortunate who perceptions are That they do not have the power to fight or who do not realize they have that power to fight for themselves is already there within them.

Dr. King was a man that believed in The God of Heaven and His way of peace.

136

He believed that all men were equal as God said, *"There is neither Jew nor Greek, there is neither bond nor free, there is neither male nor female: for ye are all one in Christ Jesus, Galatians 3:28-29." Master Study Bible, King James Version, 2001*

In contrast, there are those that believe different. The Ku Klux Klan did not believe that the black man should have any rights only those that were told them, they could have. Their mentality spread to a fever pitch and the blacks and other minorities were back almost two hundred years. When there is a need, there is always someone to fill it. Dr. King was the helper that filled that need.

The black race presented the check many times before to the Bank of freedom; it always came back just as presented, not cashed, but stamped and sent back and marked as having "Insufficient funds." *Martin Luther King, Jr., 1963.*

That freedom was not there for the blacks yet, not in a manner that they could enjoy, not quite yet.

Even the recognition that the black race had the same rights the United States Constitution afforded every citizen just was not there. An ideology is far more dangerous than the actual act. Ideologies starts in the minds of humans and the only way to change it is to change the human's mind, which is hard to do, because change comes hard; here again, is that idea of "Status Quo", if it ain't broke don't fix it. The Ku Klux Klan did not think or believe that the system of justice was broken, especially not for the black race, and it definitely did not need fixing.

King (1963) said at the foot of the Lincoln Memorial, "I am happy to join you today in what will go down in history as the greatest demonstration for freedom in the history of our nation" I have A Dream, August 28, 1963.

From Montgomery to Selma, the heat wave of this final march and fight for "true freedom was felt." It was also, felt in Washington, D.C., the Capital of the United States. The check that was presented in the past, to the "Bank of Freedom" that was returned stamped as having "Insufficient Funds" was now being special delivered by Dr. King, and not being sent in a snail mail type manner. King stated that, "It was a Promissory Note every American falls heir too." *I have a Dream, Martin Luther King, Jr. 1963.*

According Merriam Webster (2012), an heir is one who, equally inherits or is entitled to, the property or rank of another upon that person's death. Further, an heir is a person inheriting and continuing the legacy of a predecessor. *Merriam Webster Free Dictionary, m-w.com. August 14, 2012*

An heir does not get the leftovers from an estate, no matter whether they are naturally born or adopted. If they are listed as an "Heir" it means "equal" shares of all the "rights" and "privileges" thereof.

King's march for freedom and the delivery of the unpaid checks took him to the foot, of the Lincoln Memorial where he delivered one of the greatest speeches ever made by man in this century.

"*Five score years ago, a great American, in whose symbolic shadow we stand today, signed the Emancipation Proclamation. This momentous decree became a beacon of light for millions of Negro slaves.*" I have a Dream, Martin Luther King, Jr., 1963

Four hundred years is a long time to wait for what was on paper to become a reality for a race of people and other minorities that would come hereafter.

According to King (1963), "One hundred years later the Negro is still crippled by the manacles of segregation and chains of discrimination." *I have a Dream, Martin Luther King, Jr., 1963*

The progress, of the Negro, had been impaired by, the restraints of segregation and discrimination. Restraints are chains that bind and prevent movement. The sequence of facts and events, that happened were unending for hundreds of years and then some. Slavery and Segregation are both isolation factors that caused racial lines placed in this society that were impassable. The heritage, King (1963) spoke of, that was left in the Emancipation Proclamation and Constitution of the United States by the forefathers, had not been awarded to the Negro. *I Have a Dream, Martin Luther King, Jr. August 1963*

According to King (1963) "There is no way that equal justice is so scarce that it was not enough to go around to all citizens." Banks do not go bankrupt overnight. This country was still in its youthful stage, there was no way that the Bank of justice was broke. Further, banks cannot operate without the availability of a sufficient amount of funds. Opportunity was looming everywhere. "The vault of opportunity was overflowing with rights, equality and justice", *I have a Dream, Martin Luther King, Jr., August 1963.*

The dream was there for all to enjoy even with the problems that existed. The dream to build a great and different America did not start in August 1963, the day of this thought provoking speech, but hundreds of years past. All American have the same dream, of prosperity, freedom, equal rights, justice, and above all living in peace.

In reference to equality, King (1963) said, "I have a dream that my four little children one day will live in a nation where they will not be judged by the color of their skin but by the content of their character, I have a dream today." *I Have A Dream, Martin Luther King, Jr., August, 1963.*

"This will be the day – this will be the day when all of God's children will be able to sing with new meaning, "My Country 'tis of thee, sweet land of liberty, of thee I sing, Land where my fathers died, land of the pilgrim's pride, from every mountainside, let freedom ring." Smith (1861) wrote this beautiful song. Dr. King appropriately used the words in his speech, which speaks of America as a land of liberty. Therefore, if America is to be a great nation, this must become true.

As Dr. King (1963) continued to say, "And when this happens when we allow freedom to ring: when we let it ring from every village, and every hamlet, from every state, and every city we will be able to speed up the day when all, of God's children, black men, white men, Jews and Gentiles, Protestants and Catholics will be able to join hands and sing in the words of the old Negro Spiritual, "Free at last! Free at last! Thank God almighty, we are free at last!"

I Have a Dream, Martin Luther King, Jr., August 1963

Thereby there could have been no better ending to this speech than, to be spoken with this reasoning and question, "Why all men no matter their race, creed and color, of their skin, cannot enjoy the privileges which this great nation affords them?" Especially, since, this country was hewn out and built with the blood of the citizens held in slavery and made to live on the other side of lines drawn that gave no equal rights" *I Have A Dream, Martin Luther King, Jr., August 1963.*

Abraham Lincoln, President of the United States (1863), was the first parousia. President Lincoln presented the check of equality, for payment, for the Negro race to the bank of justice, for the bank to make good on its promises of justice for all. When he penned the Emancipation Proclamation he gave freedom to a race of people who had been had been denied freedom for many years. *Emancipation Proclamation, Abraham Lincoln, 1863.*

In 1963, one hundred years later, Martin Luther King, Jr. was the second parousia. Dr. King went presenting the check to the bank of justice the second time, asking that America's bank of justice make good on the promise of justice for all and that the 13th and 15th Amendments of the Constitution be honored as written; he finally got adjudication for debt that had been long overdue.

The United States Constitution, 1776.

Like Dr. King, a futurists in another country, had a dream for freedom and equality for his people. President Nelson Mandela fought for freedom for the oppressed and the disenfranchised citizens of his country, South Africa. *Mandela, 1994.*

To further support the subjugation of blacks in the South as well as, in some of the Northern States in America, the author offers these examples from another continent around the world.

South Africa was not the only country that lines and oppressions existed. The English also bore some of the guilt of the tyranny that was heaped upon the black race even in the United Kingdom. http://www.history.ac.uk/ihr/Focus/Slavery/articles/sherwood.html, February 21, 2013

The three examples are: (1) the fight for Apartheid and President Nelson Mandela and (2) Yakubu, a Kenyan child's perspective (3) the Jungle Commission, by Author, Jomo Kenyatta in the books Things Fall Apart with Connections, by *Achebe, Chinua.*

CHAPTER 38

Lines do not usually exist only in one country; but there are lines in other countries as well, especially racial lines. Racial bias did not originate with the Ku Klux Klan. There have always been underlying factors humans blamed for racial bias and many nations that subject human to these racial biases. There is a color line drawn around the world, which includes Alabama and other southern states.

Lines not only existed in the South in America, but also in other countries and on other continents. A race of people cannot live to be their best regardless of the country or continent, where there is an inequality line to fight to get across.

Nelson Mandela lived on the other side of a line because of his fight against Apartheid (South African political system where only whites had political rights and power), *Learners Dictionary, 2012.*

Nelson Mandela said, "There is no passion to be found playing small in settling for a life that is less than the one you are capable of." *Nelson Mandela, Former President of South Africa.*

The poet, Emerson, mirroring President Nelson Mandela, said, "What lies behind us and what lies before us are tiny matters compared to what lies within us." *Ralph Waldo Emerson.*

This quote sums up what the Negro have fought for; for centuries living a life less than what they were capable of is not very attractive or encouraging. A goal equals passion. When you live by someone else's yea or nay, life has less of a futuristic meaning. It is like living in a grey area. Living in someone else's shadow dims the view of what can be or who a people can or could be; to be more specific, what the black race could be.

Shane said, "It seemed that the Ku Klux Klan used the Civil Rights Era to bring to the forefront what was already brewing below the surface and it finally spilled over into a volcano of tension and hate, flowing like volcanic ash downward destroying all in its path."

The Civil Rights Era could be called an era of opportunity for the Ku Klux Klan to carry their plan of trying to prevent the black man from having equal rights by taking their strategy to the next level. The Klan was like a voluminous volcano that erupted and kept growing in size and affecting the same types of tragedy. Like a volcano, they buried their victims under the ash of hate, bias, and deliberate destruction.

Have those racial lines gone, have they gotten better, or are they still there, looking from today's standpoint?

According to Christian (2002) along with the African American experience, there are many other examples of African Diaspora communities grappling with the legacy of White supremacy; Liverpool, England, offers one such case. Due to the city's involvement in the enslavement of African, it grew rich and became a major player in the development of the plantation economies in the Caribbean and North America.

According to Christian (2002) That is specifically in the trafficking and distribution of enslaved Africans, in the exploitation of African labor for the production of raw materials, and in the development of industries and commerce directly connected to ships that carried enslaved Africans to their destination in the New World. The city of Liverpool could not have grown in prosperity without its central government in the enslavement of Africans, *Christian, Mark, Miami University, Ohio, 2002*

According to Christian (2002) As a way of providing a platform for reconciliation in December 1999, the Liverpool City Council formally apologized for the city's participation in the trans-Atlantic enslavement era and issued a formal apology:

"On behalf of the city, the City Council expresses its shames and remorse for the city's role in this trade in human misery. The City Council makes an unreserved apology for its involvement in the slave trade and the continual effects of slavery on Liverpool's Black community."

"The first steps towards reconciliation will the basis upon which the city, and all its people and institutions can grasp the challenges of the new millennium with a fresh and sustainable commitment to equality in Liverpool." (*Journal of Black Studies*, Vol. 33 No 2, November 2002 179-198 DIO: 10.1177/002193402237224

There was always a British connection. This true-life account echoes this connection. In the British "connection" told through a fable, *The Jungle Commission*, paints a vivid picture of an all too true truth of human interactions and dealing with each other. Man seems to always want a "one-up" on their fellow man as did the animals in this account.

Yakubu, a native of the Country of Kenya, related this story to me of his experience of the events of Life of Emergency of Kenya by a Baby/Child, as he expressed it in his words.

The account of Yakubu's suffering, as a baby child, is written exactly as he related it to me. I wrote it accurately as he said it happened without any changes.

Yakubu said that, "The scars received, from his experience as a child is still with him, even today." Yakubu lives in America now and teaching in the Sciences. Yakubu is a brilliant teacher and researcher. His writings and articles are well-known in the scientific world.

Yakubu begin by saying, "Human carnages was happening everywhere in the world without respect to any geographical location; lines are drawn everywhere with respect to race, power or position.

Earlier on before I was born, some African had organized themselves into militant groups to fight against their colonial masters for their freedom. These freedom fights operated from the forests away from their opponents.

Yakubu said, "It is the events, emanating from that struggles I had that would help to shape my early life. The single event of my experience of the events of Life of Emergency in Kenya influenced me more than any other event of my life."

Yakubu's life experience and narration. "I was born in Kenya, a country located in the eastern parts of Africa sometimes in 1950's when the nation was a British Colony. All the children of my age were born at home and I too was born at home in a small homestead. It was much later in my life that I was shown the spot where our homestead stood and hence my place of birth.

A few years before the leader of the freedom fighters-Mr. Dedan Kimathi was arrested then executed by the British, the freedom fighters received a great deal of support from their country-mates who were employed as farm laborers by their European masters. The support, which was distributed at night, included spying against British, garments, food and weapons, among others."

http://www.workers.org/2007/world/kenya February 22, 2013

As a result, the farm employees exercised double loyalty by serving their colonial masters, faithfully, in the day but hosting their forest based freedom fighters at night. Therefore, it was the same people, who ensured that the movement recruited more young people by administering some oaths as a symbol of loyalty to their cause.

However, as in other settings of life, such help would occasionally leak to the employer who would ensure that the betrayals received corresponding punishments-"canning" them in public. I think this was the most demeaning punishment that the colonial masters handed their subjects.

Yakubu said, "It was a very brutal and traumatizing experience, to us children, seeing a grown up being *canned* in public and more so because no African would have done that to another African in open. Scenes of that nature scarred us and forced us to run away and hide in the small huts that we called our homes. Besides, after punishing them, the farm owner would then hand them over to Government authorities who would in turn, subject them to a jail term of many years.

At times, the law enforcement officer-the police, took matters into their own hands by deciding the nature of the punishment that was deterrent enough to stop once and, for all repetition of "a crime." Unfortunately, for most of the times, that turned out to be fatal. On one occasion, a Foreman, of the Farm was said to have cooperated with the freedom fighters. When the Senior British Officer, and his team, arrived, he pulled a dagger and approached the suspect, menacingly as the suspect sought the protection of weeping members of his family. To their shock, he pulled him forward and plunged the dagger into the suspect's thoracic cavity. The suspect died in full view of all the members of his family. Later on, the officer boasted that the suspect's life was not worth wasting a bullet on. The son of the suspect, who is also, a brother-in-law of Yakubu has re-lived that horrible day over and over again in his memory since he was a baby!

Unfortunately, these steps were taken to deter others from becoming "copy-cats" and copying what was then considered as "a wrong example".

Unfortunately, at times, the forest-based freedom fighters would not know when it was not safe to continue their night visits or when their hosts were in jail. In other occasions, they would mistakenly, attempt to recruit new members who may have been a collaborator of the British. It was after such occasions when their visits would fail to accomplish their missions of rewarding them with their expectations.

The freedom fighters felt betrayed, as a result, of which they punished the farm employees using any means possible. It was after such one incident that had resulted in arresting of one freedom fighter by the employer when I witnessed a horrifying experience. We were all asleep in the late hours of the night when I was awaken by the commands of one of the freedom fighter who was saying; "Choma yote" some Swahili-commands -our language meaning-burn all of them.

Yakubu said that, "My father lifted me up and hosted me on his neck then carried my baby sister on his back. The incident had overtaken our mother so much that she could hardly walk. My father kept yelling at her-Wambui-her maiden name-run faster. We escaped to safety by fleeing to the guarded shed of the daily cows of the farm owner that were guarded by security guards. The results were devastating. Our neighbors were not as lucky. Although I was not big enough to know the implications of deaths, I witnessed the charred remains of my playmates- a horrifying experience that I have lived with to this day.

It was after that incident of burning, the homesteads that all the farm workers and their families were herded into some concentration camps. The small huts had their walls covered with mud. The roofs were grass-thatched. It was in one of those huts where all the members of one family were made to live in. My parents, like nearly all other African employees who were working in that farm lived in one of them.

Our parent's bed, was separated from an open sight, with a sisal gunny bag. By the time I had gained some realizations, of some kind, we were all living in these grass-thatched huts. All around these settlements were high barbed wire fences and behind the barbed wire fences were deep tunnels- six to ten feet deep.

Indeed, since then, I have seen movies depicting the way Nazi Germany treated their captives. I do not think that there existed much difference in the life, we too lived. Yakubu said, "As I write this account, three survivors of this brutality are in London pursuing a legal settlement against the British."

Whenever there has been a hearing, the attendee had been shocked to learn of the atrocities committed by colonial masters at the watch of the British administrators.

Yakubu's account of his life experiences as a child can be compared or contrasted to the story, "The Jungle Commission" written in the book, All Things Fall Apart with Connections, by Chinua Achebe. These stories are written as a fable; however, they can also, apply to life and the way humans deal with each other.

In the short story, The Jungle Commission, by Jomo Kenyatta. There is a quote in this story that mirror what was taking place all over the South during the, Civil Rights Era. Kenyatta (1958) said, "*Ng'enda thi ndeagaga motegi,*" which literally means, "There is nothing that treads on the earth that cannot be trapped," in other words, you can fool people for a time, but not forever; peace is costly, but it's worth the expense." p 204. *Achebe, Chinua: Things Fall Apart with connections.*

No matter how elusive you are there is entrapment for any living being on earth. There is a scorecard in every society that rate human relations in difference and race and as to whether there is positive-growth, in those relationships.

Looking finally, at a Score Card of progress, in America in regards to race. The 2008 Presidential Election is the example that this author chose to use to support the question of race in America.

CHAPTER 39

Our scorecard, our rating now, what is it?

We live in a two-door society, with both doors open. Those doors can be problematic. We do not need to close but one of them. We cannot close the door on America's past, but we can close that part of that door on racism, inequality, injustice and the racial division in our nation. The other part of that door need to be left open, reminding each of us where we were and where we have come from and what we have come too, and where we need to go as a nation and a society. The door that is labeled equality and justice, which demands a united front against oppression and those who would oppressed should always be open.

To close that door of inequality, injustice and racial division, in our nation will take all the citizens of this great country. With each of us taking hold and pushing together that doors of inequality, injustice and racial division aside that has stood like a wall between the door of equal rights and fair treatment, of all no matter who they are. To start the door moving toward closure, it will start with each of us and using the multiplier effect adding one more person pushing for freedom and justice each time the multiplier moves around adding one more person each time until all Americans are pushing together as one. The multiplier effect works well, *Schiller (2009), Essentials of Economics p.265, 341.*

Moreover, passing the cookie to the powers to be and leaving the crumbs to the rest is passing like time. It is history. Human rights, the full array of them is crying out to all and for all.

The door that reminds us of that negative part of our past that has long-ago become irrevocable can be seen as being still yearned for and held onto by erecting statues.

Nathan Bedford Forrest, a known Ku Klux Klan leader, supporters are trying to erect a permanent statue to his honor. Presently, the statue had been stolen, and being replace with tighter security. This ideology and mentality still exists. With all the injury and harm this ideology caused citizen in Selma and the surrounding areas, as well as, state and country will set as a constant reminder with this statue being in place. It is unbelievable after more than sixty years people still hold on to the past. This article appeared in the news and on a video: Who in the? Alabama is Building a Monument to Honor KKK Founder. The Black community in Selma fought against the building of this monument. http://globalgrind.com/news/selma-al-build-monument-honoring-kkk-founder-Nathan–bedf, August 24, 2012

Example of the second Scorecard is the November 5, 2008 Presidential Election. To summarize, how was the election, of President Barack H. Obama Framed?

The Scorecard of the Framing of a President, November 5, 2008. This project was assigned to the researcher by a Professor of the Communication Department at the University of South Alabama. The author of this book used this analogy as an example to look at the scorecard and opinions of a Presidential Elections in this country.

The researcher conducted this study over a period of six month. The Final Analysis of the November 5, 2008 Presidential Election was submitted, May 2009.

The results of the Framing of the Presidential Election November 5, 2008.

The researchers' findings as follows:

Framing of a President

In the study, of the Newspapers for the Framing of the Presidential Election, the researcher expected to find that Newspapers across America would be fair and impartial in their coverage of the election the day after the election November 5, 2008.

The Newspaper Headlines examined were to determine if the majority of the Newspapers reported the election results without "racial" biases being factors in the tone of their analyses or the results of the coverage.

The results of the study proved that the majority of the Newspapers were blatantly racial; used very strong racial innuendoes; or painted a racial picture of the election for their audiences, the American public, using racial signs or symbolic language.

Did the media Frame depict events in ways that constrain how their audiences can interpret the event? The media interaction with what the public thought processes are creates a public agenda, of what they should think or believe.

The focus of this study is to determine how the Newspaper Headlines across America framed the Presidential Election November 5, 2008, the day after the election, November 6, 2008. The researcher coded the data: Category 1 (Racial victory) Category 2 (Democratic/Political victory) and Category 3 (Neutral).

Firstly, the headlines that depicted the Presidential Election results as a victory, for the African-American Race, the researcher placed in the Racial Category.

Secondly, the headline that depicted the Presidential Election results as Democratic/Political the researcher placed in the Democratic/Political category.

Thirdly, the headlines that did not depict the Presidential election in either of the categories racial or political, the researcher placed in the Neutral category.

The Methodology used was Content Analysis to study the Newspapers election results.

The Sample Population used was the headlines of the daily Newspapers across America and abroad. For the study, the researcher used Seven Hundred Thirty-five Newspapers (735).

A Purposive Sample was taken from the Seven Hundred Thirty-Five front pages of the Newspapers throughout America and abroad.

The researcher selected every tenth (10th) front page of the Newspapers from both nationally and internationally; which included the secondary headlines of the seventy-three Newspapers used in the study. The archives used were the http://www.newseum.org . November 2009

The remainder of the front pages not used in this study, were from International Newspapers or; they were not suitable for use for this study. Also in the analysis, there were Newspaper publications that did not provide headlines of the election coverage on November 5, 2008. If there were no headlines on the front page the researcher discarded these Newspaper samples.

The remainder of the Newspapers that did not fit into one of the three categories were not useable because of language differences (see paragraph for additional information).

After the preliminary elimination was completed, the researcher used random selections from the sample News Headlines used in the study. Ten newspaper headlines and secondary headlines with quotes from Category 1 (Racial); five newspaper headlines and secondary headlines with quotes from Category 2 (Democratic/Political) and three newspaper headlines and secondary headlines with quotes from Category 3 (Neutral). (See Example Chart and Graphs)

The Findings:

Forty-six of the Newspaper headlines fit into Category 1 (Racial). Twelve of the Newspapers headlines fit into Category 2 (Democratic/Political). Six of the Newspaper headlines fit into Category 3 (Neutral), and the other eight were not usable.

Examples

Category 1 – Racial

In Our Lifetime: Obama Sweeps to victory makes history as the first black President. Wire report, "The nation that in living memory struggled violently over racial equality will have its next President a 47-year old, one term U.S. Senator born of a Kenyan father rand Kansan mother." (*Anniston Star, November 5, 2008*).

Change on the Horizon: Obama elected first black president. Koskey and Young (2008) "Barack Obama, riding a wave of economic discontent with the wind of history at his back, was elected as the nation's first black President Tuesday night in a sweeping victory that stretched from the deep south to the frontier west, ending eight years of Republican rule and beginning a new era in America complex racial history." *(Appeal–Democrat, November 5, 2008)*.

Obama's the one: Clear victory for the nation's first black President. Holman and Kranisk (2008) reporting for the Boston Globe states that" Senator Barack Obama of Illinois was elected the 44th President of the United States and the nation's first black Commander and Chief Tuesday, his triumph ushering in an era of profound political and social realignment in America." (*Record-Journal, November 5, 2008*).

President Obama: Landslide for first black chief executive. Dinan, Beltone and Caul (2008) wrote, " Mr. Obama, a 47-year old son of a Kenyan father and a Kansan mother defeated Republican John McCain to become the nation's first black President-elect and in doing so also reshaping the electoral map on the strength of historic turnout among both enthusiastic young and minority voters. (*Washington Times, November 5, 2008*).

Obama Wins: Senator Break racial barriers, take Presidency. Associated Press (2008) wrote, "Obama stepped through a door opened 145 years ago when Abraham Lincoln, a fellow Illinois Politician freed African –Americans from enslavement in the rebellious South in the midst of a wrenching Civil War. (*Florida Today, November 5, 2008*).

YES, HE DID! A singular day in American History. (*The Tampa Bay Times, (tbt), November 5, 2008*)

OH-Bama! America elects its first Black President. Espo (2008) wrote, "Barack Obama sweeps to victory as the nation's first black President Tuesday night in an electoral landslide that overcame racial barriers as old as America itself." *(Kennebec Journal, November 5, 2008).*

OBAMA IN THE HOUSE! (*The Trentonan, November 5, 2008*).

Barack OBAM A! Barack claims Presidency in historic election. "Democratic Presidential nominee Senator Barack Obama battled Republican candidate Senator John McCain for the support of American voters Tuesday, creating history to become the first minority to become the nation's President-elect." (*The Brownsville Herald, November 5, 2008*).

Barak Obama makes history, A New Face of America: Black Senator from Chicago elected U. S. President. Goodman (2008) writes, "Barack Obama was swept to the White House on Tuesday by in captured Americans who embraced the message of hope and turned their backs on centuries of racial divisions by electing the first black President." (*The Sudbury Star, November 5, 2008*).

Category 2 (Democratic/Political)

OBAMA WINS: Defeats McCain in Indiana, Ohio; Grabs GOP stronghold, swings states; Democrats widen congress majorities. Shear and Baines (2008) wrote, "Obama becomes the first Democrat since Jimmy Carter in

1976 to receive more than 50 percent of the popular vote, and made good on the pledge to transform the Electoral Map." (*The Journal Gazette, November 5, 2008*).

YES, HE DID! Good Night to Be a Democrat. Boshart (2008) "Democrat Barack Obama, turned Iowa from red to blue in an impressive fashion Tuesday en route to becoming the first African American to be elected President of the United States. (*The Gazette, November 5, 2008*).

OBAMAWINS: Democratic Senator claims majority victory as United States elects its first Black President. Pickler (2008) of the Associates Press wrote, "A triumphant Barack Obama vowed on Tuesday night to be the President for all America." *(Daily News, November 5, 2008)*.

OBAMA WINS: Historic Triumph. Democrat invokes the words of Lincoln and Kennedy as he talk of challenges ahead. Espo (2008) writes, "On a night for Democrats to savor they not only elected Obama the nation's 44th President, but padded the majorities in the house and senate, and come January will control both the White House and the Congress for the first time since 1994." (*New Hampshire Union Leader, November 5, 2008*).

Historic Win for Obama. Democrats capture Presidency in landmark election, major victory reflects change in campaigns demographics and political order of states. Thomas (2008) wrote, "Barack Obama was elected the 44th President of the United States on Tuesday, swept to victory by an anxious country eager to change course at home and abroad." (*Akron Beacon, November 5, 2008*).

Category 3 (Neutral)

The Christian Science Monitor reported the news as "usual" on November 5, 2008, the day after the election with the only reference to the election written in a photo inset that read; the 2008 election "Monitor Coverage of Election results is available on CSM website.

Change comes to America – Voters take leap of faith on untested leader with a bold vision. (*The Hamilton Spectator, November 5, 2008*).

Bluffton Votes: Barak Obama in Command. Morris (2008) reports that, "at press time Tuesday Night, Barack Obama was widening his electoral lead over John McCain on the historic U. S. Presidential race. But the fat lady had not sung." (*Bluffton Today, November 5, 2008*).

Framing of a President
(Pie Chart 1)

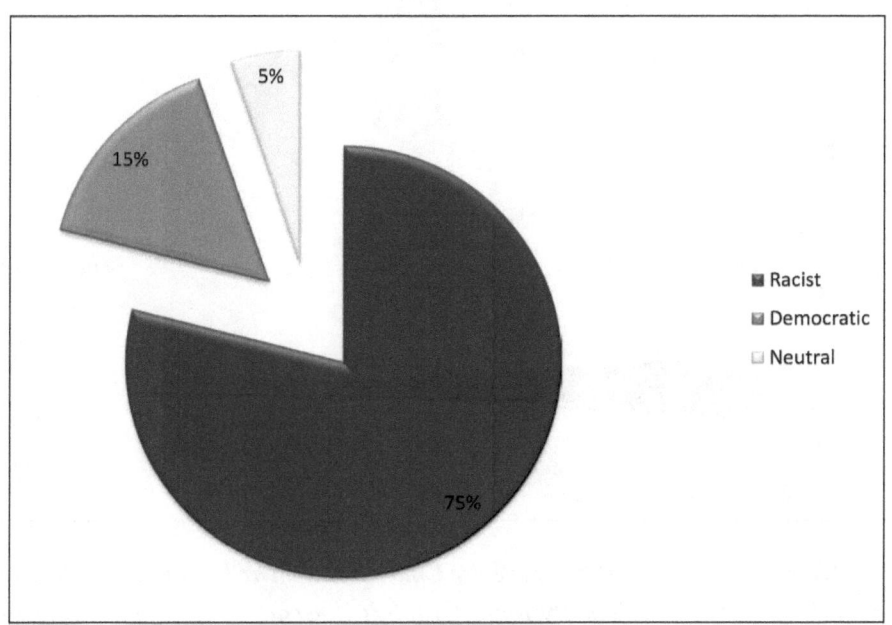

Comparing Pie Chart 1 with Graph 1

The Pie Chart is illustrative of the percentages of the different categories of the Newspapers reporting of the Presidential Election, November 5, 2008. 75% (Republican Party color, Red) of the Newspapers were categorized as Racist; 15% of the Newspapers (Democratic Party color, Blue) were categorized as Democratic/ Political; and 5% (Yellow, representative of neither Democratic nor Republican showed only that there were not an opinion the day of the election) was categorized as being Neutral.

Pyramid Graph 1
Comparative Analysis

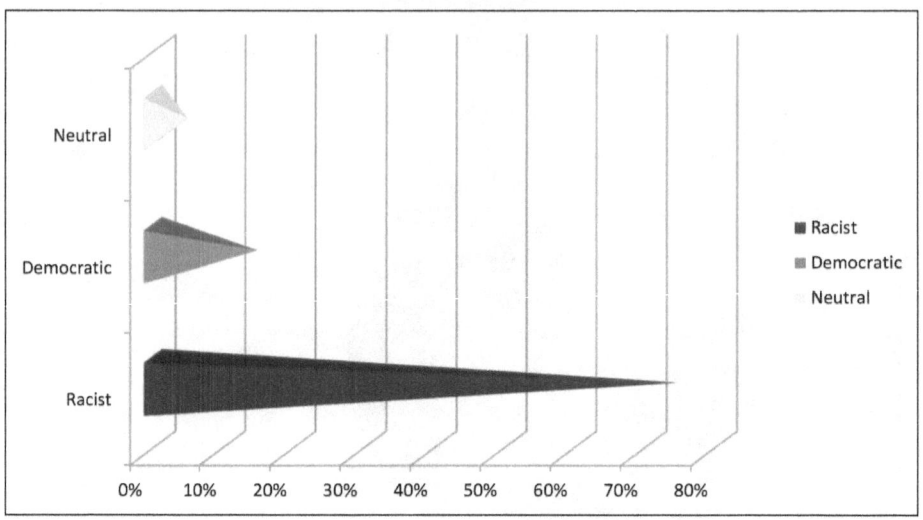

The comparative analysis of the Pie Chart 1 and 3 bar Pyramid Graph shows the analysis is the same. The Pyramid Graph is illustrative of the percentages of the different categories of the Newspapers reporting of the Presidential Election, November 5, 2008. 75% (Republican party color, Red) of the Newspapers were categorized as Racist; 15% of the Newspapers (Democratic party color, Blue) were categorized as Democratic; and 5% (Yellow, is representative of neither Democratic nor Republican showed that there was not an opinion on the day of the election was categorized as being Neutral.

The samples from each of the categories the researcher used in the analysis are shown (see Pie Chart 1 and Pyramid Graph 1).

The International Newspapers that picked up the election on the Newswire were coded in the same categories but are not show graphically since their level of significant to this study was not deemed percentage wise to be graph-able. The Newspapers used from the International sources were also categorized as: Category 1 (racial); Category 2 (Democrat/Political); and Category 3 (Neutral).

The researcher found that there were front page coverage of the election from Puerto Rico to Israel; the Newspapers cheered the win of Barack Obama, painted the election of an African-American as skeptical; and also there was in their reporting, an air of uncertainty about the new leader of the greatest nation in the world.

The remainder of the front-page category samples looked at was neutral. There were only facts reported by International Newspapers no subjectivity was used.

The researcher had assistance in interpreting the International papers of which pictures and symbols on these Newspaper fronts spoke louder than words.

Data Analysis of the Framing of a President

A prominent Southern Newspaper, The Anniston Star, depicts the nation in a struggle over racial equality. The South is portrayed as having the larger problem with the fact that, racial inequality still exists; the polls on election night supported this fact.

The first paragraph of the article written notes that, "Barack Obama is a black man", born of a Kenyan father and a Kansan mother; it was not mentioned that she was Caucasian. The Washington Times had similar views in reporting the election coverage mentioning that the President's father was Kenyan and mother Kansan.

There are no basis in fact to support the ideology that this nation is beginning another era of complex racial history, but can it be said that the nation is beginning another era of America's history, not just racial history, as supposed by the Appeal-Democrat?

America is not fighting to free blacks from slavery (this was written into Law in 1865 by Abraham Lincoln), but another kind of slavery has beset this nation in the form of economic disparity and terroristic activities, which affects all people of different races, creeds, color or natural origins.

The Washington Times (2008) reporters writes that, "The electoral map is being reshaped by the historic turnout of the young and enthusiastic minority voters." The statement made was viewed as being a left turn for the nation, a wrong turn. Reference was made only to the young and minority voters in America in the reshaping of the electoral map, not this younger generation as

155

a whole." Had not this nation been in the midst of a wrenching war between the states, Abraham Lincoln would not have freed the slaves; had there been no war, then there would be no reason for freeing the slaves; Abraham Lincoln only freed the slaves out of desperation.

According to, Florida Today, "Slavery still existed until President-elect Barack Obama stepped through a door that was opened 145 years ago." This mirrors the opinion of the Appeal-Democrat with the reference to racial equality.

The Tampa Bay Times (tbt) in special election coverage: a close-up of President Obama's face darned the front of the Newspaper. The coverage never mentioned race, but the implications are there with the single photo and the secondary headlines that reads, "A singular day in American History." Therefore, the Seventy-five Newspapers coverage's, of the November 5th election was interpreted by the Researcher, in two ways: (1) the election of a black man for President has never happened before; and (2) the electing a black man for President will never happen again.

The word singular is defined as "only or one." *Online Dictionary, November 2009*

The one and only time that Obama would be President and the one and only Black Man that will ever be chosen as President or Commander in Chief, of the United States. Racial barriers still existed in the mind of the writer; up to the point of this election, the racial barriers, had not been over-come as reported by the Kennebec Journal.

In comparison, the front-page, of the Trentonan reports: OBAMA IS IN THE HOUSE. The photo in this frame pictures Obama standing in front of the White House, clearly a black man in a white environment.

The American flag was shown not as a prominent feature, it is pictured very "small." The report seemed to indicate that it is an un-American act to place a black man in the "White" House, the photo resounds very loudly: white power vs. black power. "Obama is in the House" is a phrase that is kindred to the black culture.

The Brownsville Herald framed the election by starting their headlines: O BAM A! Barack claims Presidency in historic election. The "O" and "A" in Obama's name are white and the BAM in the middle is yellow. The writer painted a picture using symbols that indicated that he is neither white nor black but non-the-less a minority.

The headline puts a new twist on the framing of the election. The President is not a black man, yet he is a minority. The headlines positions him as being in the middle, leaving a question of which race is he in? The headlines clearly showed the racial predisposition. The BAM is between the O and the A. Both the alphabets "A" and "O" are white.

The Newspapers not only use words to picture the President in relation to race; but, also demonstrated the election in reference to race in a very picturesque and symbolic depiction. The Sudbury Star, used symbols also in their Framing of the Presidential Election. Barack Obama makes history: New face of America. Obama swept to the White House by "encaptured" Americans who just the day of the election turns their backs on centuries of racial division.

The photo caption did not picture President Obama only those labeled as "encaptured Americans. The encaptured Americans pictured were all black. Who were turning their backs on racial division? In this reference, who were the "they" being spoken, of as electing their first black President. Barack Obama is the President, of all the people. The President of the United States was elected by, the majority of the people not only black people or people of the African-American race or descent. Can only black be encaptured by another black? The Presidential Campaign proved differently as to who can be encaptured? All races were captivated by Barack Obama President Elect, of the United States, not just the black or minority race.

In contrast, the Journal Gazette framed the election as a Democratic victory, with the headline reading: Obama Wins. Defeats McCain in Indiana and Ohio; Grabs GOP Stronghold, swing states; Democrats widen Congress Majorities. The report was judicial and impartial. The Gazette framed Obama as the first Democrat since Jimmy Carter who received more than 50% of the popular vote.

The photo and caption only states that, "President-elect Barack Obama looking into the crowd after his acceptance speech in Grant Park in Chicago-the photo only reflects the poise of a victor with red, white, and blue flashes of patriotic symbols surrounding him – a picture of an American President not a black President.

In this depiction, the Journal Gazette used the symbols in a positive manner, with no racial overtones. The Gazette mirrors the Journals framing of the Presidential Election. **YES, HE DID,** are the headlines: It is a good night to be a Democrat. Barack Obama turned Iowa Blue. A very difficult state to read and swings red, white, and blue in an impressive fashion en route to becoming, the first African-American to be elected President of the United States. The photo positions Barack Obama in a victorious wave of an elected President of the people, not as an African-American President.

The victorious wave is no different from any other Presidential victors on November 5th. The 2nd Tuesday, of the Presidential Electoral Month. The secondary headlines reads: "It is a good night to be a Democrat, not a good night to be a black Democrat." This reporter took an unbiased stance in reporting the election returns. Here, only the facts were reported and these facts were not tainted by a subjective viewpoint. The Daily News writes that Obama Wins: Democrat Senator claims major victory.

The President-elect was framed as, a President that wanted to unite the country. He is the President of all the people not the President of a particular race of people. This is in direct contrast to the innuendoes of the Appeal-Democrat and the Florida Today Newspapers that he is a President of the black race only.

The New Hampshire, Union Leader publication read: OBAMA WINS. Historic Triumph. Democrat invokes the words of Presidents Lincoln and Kennedy as he talks of challenges ahead. The victory was framed as Democratic and juxtaposed with Presidents Kennedy and Lincoln who both in their administration faced daunting tasks as Presidents: Kennedy with the Cuban Missile Crisis; and Lincoln facing the War Between the States and how to unify the country.

Obama faced both Kennedy's war and Lincoln's effort to unite the country. In the war of the recession, and the prosperity of this country and the underlying factors, of how he will unite the country with an effort to "change" the direction of the United States to be more united nation and move in a noticeably positive direction would prove to be a daunting task.

The Akron Beacon Journal frames the election as a "historic" win for Obama a Democrat, captures the Presidency in a landmark election, a major victory reflects change in the campaign as well as the demographics and the political order of the states.

The Democrats were acknowledged as being, the victors in this election coverage. The election was historic in that the Democratic Party had taken back seats that had been Republicans, for more than a decade; and now the Democrats are all front-runners again signifying a unified win.

Category 1 and category 2 are directly opposite in the framing of the Presidential election. The difference in perspectives of some of the major Newspapers across the country is amazing, especially since some are in the same part of the country or just cites apart or even possibly streets apart.

The Christian Science Monitor reported the news as "usual" on November 5th the day after the election. The only reference to the election was written in a photo inset that read: The 2008 election" Monitor coverage of election results is available on the website.

The researcher offers these reasons why the Monitor and any other major Newspaper may not have framed the election results in any of the categories. The paper could have gone to press before the election results hit; or the Newspaper kept a neutral stance on the election without telling the American citizens how they should perceive the results of the November 5th election; or they could have been in direct competition with another Newspaper preferred by readers.

In comparison, the Hamilton Spectator simply reads "Change Comes to America." The Spectator framed the election in a neutral way. The Newspaper did not offer any opinion about the election results; nor did it report the election as either racial or democratic.

The Bluffton reported that Bluffton Votes: "Barack Obama in Command." The reporting was neutral. There is no mention of race or political party in this reporter's article. Only the facts, in reference to the election, were reported as the results came in.

In conclusion, the researcher found that the majority of the U.S. Daily Newspapers, the day after the election framed the Presidential election as Racial (Category 1). Newspapers that framed the election as Southern or Republican (conservative viewpoints) and the plight of the minority, are not an important factor in the success of our country, just the rich and those that have.

The Example Chart 1, Election Framing (see attached) is supportive of the researcher's findings. The findings were that, the majority of the Newspapers framed the election as being racial. Category one (C1): ten of the forty-six (the analysis only used ten of the forty-six because of the amount of space allotted) front pages framed the election as Racial; Category two (C2): five of the eight framed the election as Democratic; and Category three (C3): three of four was neutral in the framing of the election results.

Chart 1
Election Framing

Chart 1 Framing of a President		C 1 Racial Victory	C 2 Democratic/ Political Victory	C 3 Neutral
Newspapers				
Anniston Star		X		
Appeal-Democrat		X		
Record-Journal		X		
Washington Times		X		
Florida Today		X		
Tampa Bay Times		X		
Trentonan		X		
The Brownsville Herald		X		
The Kennebec Journal		X		
The Sudbury Star		X		
The Journal Gazette			X	
The Gazette			X	
Daily News			X	
New Hampshire Union Leader			X	
Akron Beacon			X	
Christian Science Monitor				X
The Hamilton Spectator				X
Bluffton Today				X
The Chart mirrors the explanation of the Analysis of a Framing of a President				

In business when dealing with products marketing strategies, become brands with which can to be associated when buying or using a product; thereby, creating a brand loyalty. Some of the Newspapers used the words Southern or Republican in the reporting of the election results; this is a brand that the Republicans have created for themselves. Could this be a marketing strategy used by the Republican Party? This is a constant irritant, that could be used to keep the Democrat Party on their toes or on the run. This author see the this as the Republicans picturing themselves for the public as being the right party to be identified with because they are the "right" way when looking at a political party.

Analogy by *Carlotta Maria Shinn-Russell, University of South Alabama Masters of Communication Program, May 2009.*

Finally, are we as a country moving forward? In this case, what is the pace? Is it at a slow pace or is it at a fast past?

Those are some of the questions, that each American should ask themselves when, thinking of race and equality.

Therefore the quest continues. It is like climbing a mountain you are nearing the top, almost there, but not there yet.

In this light, we come to the conclusion, of Shane Washington, as she saw the Civil Rights Movement in her eyes as a child.

CHAPTER 40

In conclusion, history has a teaching factor. The Scripture tells us that, "We learn from past generations. According to Roman 15:4: For whatsoever things were written aforetime were written, for our learning that we through patience and comfort of the scriptures might have hope. *Master Study Bible, King James Version, 2001*

In this wise, man as a whole seem to never learn from past-history and the events that have taken place in this country, as well as, other continents even before this country was ever founded.

The Egyptians put the Jews in bondage, for more than four hundred years until a leader was, identified by God. He was a leader who grew into manhood among the Egyptian people; his named was Moses. Moses became a Prince of Egypt. Pharaoh's Daughter named him Moses upon drawing him from the Nile River, Exodus 2: 1-22. "Take this baby and nurse him for me, and I will pay you." So the woman took the baby and nused him. When the child grew older, she took him to Pharoah's daughter and he became her son. She named him Moses, Saying, "I drew him out of the water." Exodus 2:8-10, *Master Study Bible, King James Version, 2001*

Also, the Jews were in bondage in the Persian Empire for more than eighty years. Under the reign of King Nebuchadnezzar II, the Babylonian Empire spread throughout the Middle East, and around 607 B.C., King Jehoiakim of Judah was forced into submission, becoming a vassal to Nebuchadnezzar. 2 Kings 24:1 *Master Study Bible, King James Version, 2001*

The Europeans, the first Pilgrims to come to America, were in bondage under the King of England. They did not have the privilege to make their own choice as to how they wanted to worship and whom they chose to worship. The pilgrims suffered religious persecution before they left England. The Religious beliefs, for the people of England were decided by the King or the Royal Throne; religion loyalties of the people were to the Church of England or else. Religious freedom was not a choice they could make. *http://www. history.ac.uk/reviews/review/192*

The Europeans and Americans put the Indians on a Reservation, which is a type of bondage. Their privileges were gone to roam freely and possess their land, as they had done for more than Ten Thousand Years on this continent.

Americans went all the way to Africa to import slaves to America and auction them off on an auction block in the South. In Mobile, Alabama there is a plaque and a marker where the slaves were sold for money to be put on plantations and used like beast of burden to be put under the "lash" as a means of managing human flesh. http://www.google.com/search?hl=en&output=search&sclient=psy-ab&q=slavery+plaque+in+Mobile%2C+Alabama+&btnK

All of the lines of race and color that were old, whether it was the Jews in slavery, under the Pharaoh, the Jews in slavery under the Persian Empire, the blacks taken from Africa to become slaves to plantation owners in the South, which was all physical slavery, and the Native Americans put on reservations another sort of slavery. In addition to the physical slavery, there were emotional, social, and mental slavery going on at the same time. The mental and emotional strength of humans can be broken less easily than the physical. So therefore, slave owners had to break slaves at all levels at the same time.

Even with, the breaking of their emotional and physical strength among these; there is still one strength that no man can break. Humans have a need for the connection with a higher power, a power unseen; the power of God. That is one thing that all slaves had in common was "Hope" you cannot see hope, nor break hope. Hope is emotional and mental, unseen and protected from a master's whip.

There is but one cure for hope and that is "hope" realized. All the years that bondage held black people, they never gave-up on hope for freedom. Freedom is important to every living being, even the animal species. There should be no lines for man to have to avoid traversing.

The Native Americans, original inhabitants of this land, was too, put in bondage and labeled "Savage", which created a double line for them to cross. The reservations the Native American, the indigenous people, of this country were put on were no more than wastelands. In this regard, the Native Americans were left without the ability to secure a living, for themselves on these wasteland reservations. They were slaves to an ideology that the immigrants to America bought with them.

Lines drawn, regardless of where they are or for whom they are drawn, are dehumanizing. God created man to have the ability to make choices in their lives of the how, where, when, what, and who. One man should not have the right to put another under any type of bondage or slavery using them as beast of burdens.

The generations that will come after will learn from the previous actions of their ancestors and, if we are not careful, they will carry the torch lit bright and marching forth with the ideology of their ancestors. Changing the color of a person's skin, which seems to be a line, is not possible.

People cannot change their race, color or natural origin. There is only one way to advance the race or color line; why not cross that line and learn about the people, and their culture. Put down our innate habits to judge others and look at others through someone else's eyes.

There have been so many nations and races of people subjected to slavery since the world begin, should make man stop and think. History reports to us that none was ever completely successful. There were always, intervening factors which changed the conditions, for the race of people being in subjection to the slavery at that time.

Humans no matter where they are or the conditions which subjects them at that time, will always have the hope and desire to live free in this country and throughout the world. Living without constraints of any form of slavery imposed by another human being is the true meaning of being free, because slavery draws lines.

The lines are disappearing, just as the lines with time and repairing of the Georgetown-Chunchula Road, disappeared. Those were physical lines, which are far less dangerous than the emotional, social, and mental lines. Humans must change their ideology and way of thinking about other races and let justice and equal rights prevail. Therefore, each of us will have to let that elimination start with 'self", the face you see in the mirror every day.

What face do you see in the mirror? Is it the face of change?

Shane said, "It was my desire and belief that, for me to have any semblance of life, I would have to get past the pain and hurt I suffered as a child while watching my parents and other neighbor's dignity being mishandled by members of the white race, because they could. As well as the Ku Klux Klan inciting them from behind the scenes urging people on with their hate and racist propaganda. The Ku Klux Klan was like a fire across the South, destruction lay everywhere in the wake of their passing. A fire destroys leaving only ashes behind. I knew that only I could change my thinking and learn to forgive."

She continued, after a long moment of silence and said, "I won't say forget, because you can't; it stands as a vanguard going before so you will always remember why going forward with building human relationships are important and not let the racial issues and the past hold me hostage, which is a bondage in and of itself."

Race issues are loaded guns with the past ever standing as a Watchman. The past, teaches you how to deal with those race or line issues if they ever come up. It is all up to the person how they deal with a race issue or defuse that race issue. Shane told me that, "She left this behind long years ago and it has bode-well for her personally."

Shane said that, "She thought about how difficult it was for her family and other families in their community with just the fear, mental and emotional effects of this period. Living afraid everyday as a child is unbearable, but how much worse it must have been on the ones that suffered the physical abuse and threats along with the mental and emotional abuse. Not only in the 1960's, during The Civil Rights Movement, but since the beginning time when human bondage started and the scandalous treatment of other humans in regards to respect, equality and justice comes from the heart."

As time passes, and as you live and grow and experience life and people, you learn to live in the world as it is. Changing your way of thinking will change the feelings of bitterness, hate and resentment. A change comes only from the willingness of the people to change. Change comes only with education, understanding, knowledge, and acceptance of the others, no matter their race or color of their skin. The only way to eliminate that spiral of silence is a start with self and work from the inside out.

That "Old white man" Ku Klux Klan's ideology and tight grip on the throat of the black race saw the beginning of its end during the 1960's Civil Rights Movement. This "Old White man's" ideology and way, of power have been bull-dozed off the highway into the ditch of "enough". This kind of ideology, set in the 1960's, would not encroach itself upon a race of people any longer. The ticking clock of "need" for justice, equality and freedom was nearing its midnight and daybreak was upon the new ideology of freedom and justice for all. The mist that once hung, as a blanket over a race of people was gone, sight and vision appeared on the horizon of justice and equality for all. The political squeeze that been Chairman of the Board of this ideology, for so long had been voted-out by and replace by the committee called a "Need" for justice.

America's symbol of justice at every court and judge's bench wears a blind fold. Justice is blind; it does not look through eyes of color, natural origin, belief or values; but justice, for all, and justice are based-upon, the rights and the laws designed for everyone not for a specific race (s).

Martin Luther King, Jr., was the boots-on-the-ground freedom fighter. He got out there and pushed against that wall that had stood so strong and tall for so long until it came down. The wall of injustice and inequality that had stood in the highway of justice for hundreds of years was finally coming down brick-by-brick.

If a nail that is being driven into a of solid oak wood is hit with a hammer long enough and hard enough, and with the continual pounding on the head of that nail it will slowly be driven into that piece of solid wood. He finally hammered the nail into that solid wood of ideology, the need for justice and equality for all especially for those citizens who had been denied this precious possession for so long.

In this light, justice and freedom are precious jewels to treasure and safeguard with all fervency. Martin Luther King, Jr., hammered that nail of justice on the head continually, until it penetrated that insufficient funds check that was returned all too often over the centuries.

Finally, that insufficient funds check was honored, not all at once, mind you, but, one dollar at a time each time presented until the all the amount due was beginning to be lessen. There is still an outstanding amount due; however, thankfully, at least seventy percent, of the over-due amount is slowly being honored through payments the Bank of Justice have deposited in the black minority freedom and justice account. Honoring the Constitutional promise set the tone and opened the way for all the minorities that would come hereafter to the magnificent shores of the greatest nation in the world.

A house starts with a foundation, a frame and a roof first, then the inside is finished which is the heart of the house. Man's heart has to change, man's actions, and treatment of other humans in regards to respect, equality and justice comes from the heart. A house can be ever so beautiful on the outside and inside, but the people that live there and their hearts are the defining factor (what are their hearts like?) It is the same with man. A person's physical house can be well dressed, and well kept, but what about their hearts?

Looking at today, Genocide of the races is still alive and well. Heartless, reckless people take upon themselves to rid the world of masses of people at their discretion.

Passing the cookie to the powers to be and leaving the crumbs to the rest is passing like time, it is history. Fairness, equality and justice are crying out for all.

What is your preference for justice? Will it be a side-lined type of justice or will it be a mainstream type justice? The future is here our preference for being in the count should not be "standing" on the sideline, but "moving" with the mainstream to garner success for the campaign for justice. Those unsung heroes and all those who struggled through this movement left their testimony for all to read. These testimonies are written with the blood and the sacrifices of these unsung heroes.

Each day that the sun comes us—it is another day to enjoy the freedom and equal rights you have and continue to plant seeds for future generations as we go. Thankfully, the daily march for freedom will go on.

Therefore, humans can learn these lessons from past miscalculations. We as citizens of the world can acquire this education by looking in the rear-view mirror, of America's history. History trials, errors and results are in the rear-view mirror of history. We read about it, look directly at it and still make the same blunders.

George Santayana said, "Those who cannot remember the past are condemned to repeat it."

Rome's destruction was a vast conflagration, as was the ruin of the Ku Klux Klan and their ideology; it was a vast firestorm. The Ku Klux Klan was not only a destructive conflagration physically, but also ideologically, the same fire existed as it did in Rome.

According to history, the invading army reached the outskirts of Rome, which had been left totally undefended. In 410 C.E., the Visigoths, led by Alaric, breached the walls of Rome and sacked the capital of the Roman Empire.

The Visigoths looted, burned, and pillaged their way through the city, leaving a wake of destruction wherever they went. The plundering continued for three days. For the first time in nearly a millennium, the city of Rome was in the hands of someone other than the Romans. This was the first time that the city of Rome was sacked, but by no means the last. *Independence Hall Association in Philadelphia (1942), The Fall of Rome, http://www.ushistory.org, March 9, 2013*

The Negro race was tired of giving over to the threats and intimidations of the Ku Klux Klan. In the end, God is the final judge of who has the rights and what rights. He created man on an equal footing not to lord, one race over another. The Ku Klux Klan's demise was immediate, unsuspected and catastrophic. The Ku Klux Klan was a terror, as a weapon, their power seemed infallible; but who would in their infinitesimal imagination could have foretold their sudden demise.

There is a will and a desire in every living human being that cannot be denied. It is like a thirst. The Negro race had this thirst. They had the will and desire to be free. They were a race of thirsty men in the lonely desert of denied rights and equality. Their will and thirst for freedom no matter the cost, was always there.

We all look for our El Paradisio, that upper room of freedom, where simple rights and freedoms that give pleasure and joy while here on earth, that freedom to live free of the incumbents of chains and imprisonments. What more Antepity can be demanded for peace and the rights for freedom and entrance into El Paradisio?

The Ku Klux Klan forgot one thing, even though the black race was afraid, they would fight for peace and if they fought long enough would win. In this life, freedom, cannot be attained by, a group or race, of people, by just wanting it. There has to be some action and not passive agreement. Freedom is always a long and arduous fight. The battlefield is, noticeably stained with the blood of all those fallen heroes. The loss of human lives, are always heavy, in a battle in the pursuit of freedom and equality. In contrast, even though the battle is hard and long, there are always people that are willing to stand firm, for this peace even to the point of giving their lives for justice, rights, equality, and peace.

Too Kill A Mockingbird could be a true story anywhere in the South based on the characters and their portrayal of situations with black and in neighborhoods that ran rampant like a wild fire all over the South. There are always helpers that stand no matter the danger there was a helper in this story as well.

The New Yorker's review of an age old favored novel portrayed the South and one person's stand for freedom again all odds is very thought provoking. Attus Finch, the main character in Harper Lee's novel, "To Kill A Mockingbird" is a very phenomenal story of racism and Southern Liberalism which portrays Attus Finch, the helper, as a heroic, strong, robust, forceful and herculean type advocate for the underdog. This story painted a picture of one black man and his family bludgeoned by circumstances; the circumstances of being black in a southern city with racist citizens.

As quoted in the review of the New Yorker, "If Finch were a civil rights hero, he would be brimming with rage at the unjust verdict. But he isn't. He's not Thurgood Marshall looking for racial salvation through the law. He was Jim Folsom, looking for racial salvation through hearts and minds." *http://www.newyorker. comreporting/2009/08/10/090810fa_fact_gladwell, May 11, 2012*

Shane said that, "She thought that this was the same premise that Martin Luther King, Jr. was basing his fight for Civil Rights on, not a vengeful rage but a peace effort to reach the hearts and minds of all fellow Americans in an effort to effect a change in a peaceful non-violent way. Change starts with changes in mind and heart this is the only way it bring a long-term lasting change."

However, paradoxically, many lost their lives in this fight for freedom. Because, freedom is never free, but comes at a high price. Blood is always the highest price for freedom. Therefore, we can label many as heroes, fallen heroes, whose names are written in history that cleared the path for freedom and those that would come after them in this endless fight.

Viola Liuzzo, of Chicago, Illinois, another helper, lost her life because she was a supporter of the Civil Rights Movement. She left her family and came to the South to help support the Civil Rights Movement, another unsung hero.

Viola Fauver Gregg Liuzzo (April 11, 1925-March 25, 1965), a Unitarian Universalist committed to work for education and economic justice, gave her life for the cause of civil rights. The 39-year-old mother, of five was murdered by white supremacists, after her participation in the protest march from Selma to Montgomery, Alabama. *http://www25.uua.org/uuhs/duub/articles/violaliuzzo. html, December 23, 2013*

Arguably, the 1960's-1970's was one of the most poignant ages in America's history. Not that the 1860's was not an important and notable time, yet, there were still drawbacks to this new found freedom provided by the Lincoln Emancipation Proclamation. This freedom was not so free; oh, it was on paper; that was plain enough. However, the black man was still being mocked by that same Nemesis, "Paper Freedom" in their quest, for the true freedom outlined in the Emancipation Proclamation. To live as free humans, in dignity and safety had not happened. The people of the black race wanted freedom, but did not have it yet, that freedom would be forthcoming and still out-of- reach.

Even today, some of man's bondage is self-made. Refuse to allow bitter inner thoughts to enslave you and prevent you from moving forward. The Civil Rights Era was a movement…so move! Move forward in action and thoughts, as well as, with the times…leave behind what "use" to be and "be" part of what "is", "will be" or "can be".

After the Civil Rights Movement moved forward, the black man had come to a crossroad. Each individual has to make a choice whether to stand in the same place, filled with hate and resentment or move on, putting all the hate and resentment behind them and live a productive life; continuing to lead those that will come after you in that same positive direction. Teaching through example, the principle of not expecting a handout; but rather, teaching them they are given a hand-up.

Inevitability, justice and freedom, for all citizens no matter the race were be-labored far too long. Therefore, this should forever be a caution light in our justice system, no matter the time-frame true justice will eventually came to past.

In this case, the race of people or that segment of society should not have to pay the price at the power of a stick of injustice hanging heavily over them. Whatever the cast of injustice, whether it is a physical, emotional, social or economic cast, it can be like a torture whip in the reckless hand of their fellowman.

The future is upon this great land that those unsung heroes fought and persevered to be part of and have equal rights; now, as an individual and as a race, use them. Should their faith and hope for the future have been in vain? The price has been paid so let everyone pick up the torch that has been ignited.

The flame is still burning bright so, join the race for freedom and equal rights. The starting place is voting, speaking out against injustice, inequality, not just for self, for everyone everywhere no matter the race, creed, color, or natural origin.

Therefore and all times, hereafter, the quest for freedom will continue. Are you going to be a contributor for freedom against injustice and tyranny or are you going to be a contributor for injustice and tyranny?

We each have this choice to make for ourselves!

SOURCES

Achebe, C. (1958). *Things Fall Apart With Connections*. Holt Rinehart and Winston, Harcourt Brace and Company, Austin, Texas, pp204.
Anti-Defamation League (2013). About the KKK. http://archive.adl.org

August 26, 2012

Battle of Antietam http://www.civilwar.org/battlefields/antietam.html,

February 11, 2013

Bienville Square, Downtown Mobile.

http://www.downtownmobile.org/explore_attractions.html? November 2012

Bristol and Transatlantic Slavery (2013). Port Cities Bristol.

http://discoveringbristol.org.uk/slavery/routes/from-africa-to-america/atlantic-crossing/people-taken-from-Africa/, February 24, 2013.

Buckley, L. Michael Donald Lynching 30 Years Later: Lagniappe.

http://classic.langiappemobile.com/articel.asp?, October 18, 2012

Christian, Mark. (1998). An African Centered approach to the Black British experience: With special reference to Liverpool. *Journal of Black Studies,* (28) 3, 291-308.

Christian, Mark. (1998). An African-Centered Perspective on White Supremacy. *Journal of Black Studies*, Vol. 33 No. 2, November 2002 179-1998. Civil Rights Movement

Coffey, J. (2000). Persecution and Toleration in Protestant England 1558-1689 London, Longman, 2000. http://*www.history.ac.uk/reviews/review/192* February 24, 2013.

*dictionary.reference.com/browse/**self+refuting**, January 15, 2013*

egypt-ancient-roman-conquest-and-occupation-historic, patachu.com, May, 2012.

Elwell, Baker's Commentary on the Bible. February 22, 2013.

Fort Sumter (1861) Firing on Fort Sumter. *http://www.nps.gov/hps/abpp/ battles,* October 2012

Glasow, A. H. *www.goodreads.com/author/quotes/1965567, November 25, 2012*

Glory Road, *University of Texas at El Paso, The (1966). http://gloryroad.utep. edu/home.aspx. February 21, 2013*

Green, O (2000). New York Times Review: A Raisin in The Sun,

http://www.timbooktu.com/orlgreen/raisin.htm, October 14, 2012.

Hayes, B. http://www.aaregistry.org/historic_events/view/ku-klux-klan-brief-biography

Hitler, Stalin, Nero, Caesar, & etc. *www.wikipedia.org/wik/self-refutingl-idea.* September 13, 2012.

Honi, S. (2009) Mobile Completes its African American Heritage Trail *http://www.preservationnation.org/magazine/2009/todays-news/mobile-*

african-american-trail.html . Online Only, Feb. 18, 2009.
February 24, 2013.

http//www.cail.org.all/Mischb/davkk.htm, October 10, 2012.

http//www.english.illinois.edu/maps/poets/m_r/randall/Birmingham.htm, May 15, 2012.

http//www.ourdocuments.gov.php?flash=true&doc=34, October 17, 2012

http://afroamhistory.about.com/od/timeline/htm, October 12, 2012.

http://ancienthistory.about.com/od/grecoromanmyth1/a/050410Pandora_and_ her_box_or_pithos.htm, May 15, 2012

http://ancienthistory.about.com/od/grecoromanmyth1/a/050410Pandora_ and_her_ box_or_pithos.htm, June 10, 2012

http://dictionary.reference.com/browse/rites+of+passage

http://discoveringbristol.org.uk/slavery/routes/from-africa-to-america/

atlantic-crossing/people-taken-from-africa/

http://globalgrind.com/news/selma-al-build-monument-honoring-kkk-founder-Nathan–bedf, August 24, 2012

http://masscommtheory.com/category/theory/spiral-of-silence/

http://online.wsj.com/home-page, September 27, 2012

http://www.aaregistry.org/historic_events/view/Ku-Klux-Klan-brief-biography

http://www.abrahamlincolnonline.org/lincoln/speeches/gettysburg.htm

http://www.archives.gov/exhibits/charters/declaration.html

http://www.archives.gov/historical-docs/document.html?

http://www.bbc.co.uk/history/people/adolf_hitler, February 13, 2013

http://www.constitutionalreform.org/ April 12, 2012

http://www.encyclopedia.com/topic/feudalism.aspx

http://www.encyclopediaofalabama.org/face/Article, May 12, 2012

http://www.history.ac.uk/ihr/Focus/Slavery/articles/sherwood.html,
February 2013

http://www.history.com/this-day-in-history, February 2013

http://www.history.com/this-day-in-history/president-lincoln-dies

http://www.imdb.com/title/tt0095647/

http://www.jewishvirtuallibrary.org/jsource/Holocaust/hitler_on_Jews.htmlHitler

http://www.google.com/search?hl=en&output=search&sclient=psy-ab&q=sla very+plaque+in+Mobile%2C+Alabama+&btnK=

http://www.law.cornell.edu/constitution/amendmentxv

http://www.loc.gov/rr/program/bib/ourdocs/13thamendment.html

http://www.mariamilani.com/ancient_rome/christian_persecution_Roman_empire.htm

http://www.mrlincolnandfreedom.org/inside.asp?ID=16&subjectID=2Source *December 25, 2012*

http://www.naacp.org/pages/naacp-history-medgar-evers

http://www.newyorker.comreporting/2009/08/10/090810fa_fact_gladwell,

http://www.pbs.org

http://www.poemhunter.com/poem/god-moves-in-a-mysterious-way/

http://www.senate.gov/civics/constitution_item/constitution.htm

http://www.splcenter.org/get-informed/intelligence-files/ideology/ku-klux-klan, February 13, 2013

http://www.theamericanrevolution.org/

http://www.thefreedictionary.com/effigy, November 24, 2012

http://www.usconstitution.net/const.htm, *May 13, 2012*

http://www.ushistory.org/us/54b.asp

http://www25.uua.org/uuhs/duub/articles/violaliuzzo.html, December 23, 2012

Keys, J.M. (1936). *The General Theory of Employment, Interest and Money*: Macmillan, London: pp. 33-34.

Kimathi, D. (1995). http://www.workers.org/2007/world/kenya-0222/,

King, Martin Luther, Jr. (1964) I Have A Dream.

Learners Dictionary, 2012

Donald, Michael. http://classic.langiappemobile.com/articel.asp?

October 18, 2012

Lee, Harper. (1960). To Kill A Mockingbird. J.B. Lippincott Co., Philadelphia 1960, 1st ed.

Library of Congress, The (2012). http://www.loc.gov/rr/program/bib/ourdocs/13thamendment.html, February 24, 2013.

Lowe, Jacques, et al (1964). The Kennedy Years. *Viking Press,* New York, NY, 1964.

Mandela, N, (1994). *Long Walk to Freedom:* Little Brown Company, New York, NY.

Master Study Bible King James Version (1999). *Cornerstone Bible Publishers. Nashville, TN.* May 11, 2012

The United States Constitution (1789*). The Preamble.*

Rosewood Massacre: http://www.blackpast.org/?q=aah/rosewood-massacre-1923, February 24, 2013.

Schiller, B. R. (2009). Essentials of Economics, 7e. McGraw-Hill Companies, Inc. New York, N.Y.

Sherwood, M. (2007). Britain, slavery and the trade in enslaved Africans.

Smith, S. F. (1861) *My Country Tis of Thee*

Stewart, J. (2006). *Bridges Not Walls. David Johnson, Building Relationships with Diverse Others*: McGraw-Hill Companies, Inc. New York, N.Y.

Teamoh, G., et.al (1990). *God Made Man, Man Made Slaves*: Mercer University Press, Macon, GA.

The Kennedy Years, Viking Press, 1964)

The New Yorker. ( ) To Kill A Mockingbird.

The Real Rosewood (2007). http://www.rosewoodflorida.com/, February 24, 2013.

Today in History (1836). Houston Retreats From Santa Anna's Army

University of South Alabama, McCall Library.

Collections.alabamamosiac.org February 13, 2013

Walton, R. (February 10, 2013). Pilgrim History. http://www.richmondancestry.org/pilgrim.shtml,

Wilson, E. O. (1978). On Human Nature. *Harvard University Press,* Cambridge, Massachusetts.

www.bbc.co.uk/history/british/abolition/africa_article_01.shtml, January, 2013.

www.defintion.com

www.dictionary.com

www.encyclopedia.com, November 21, 2012

www.history.com/topics/manifest-destiny, *February 13, 2013*

Yakubu, (2013) *My life Experiences in Kenya, Africa as a Baby/Child.*

Niccolò Machiavelli (1626) Definition. *http://oxforddictionaries.com/us, February 15, 2013.*

Stanford Encyclopedia of Philosophy (2005) Machiavellianism *http://plato.stanford.edu/entries/machiavelli/,* February 15, 2013.

Independence Hall Association in Philadelphia (1942) The Fall of Rome *http://www.ushistory.org, March 9, 2013*